The Story of Redemption

VOLUME 2 · 1 KINGS – PSALMS

KRISTIN SCHMUCKER & MIRANDA MAE EWING

Contents

05   1 KINGS

21   2 KINGS

39   1 CHRONICLES

57   **2 CHRONICLES**

83   EZRA

91   NEHEMIAH

101   ESTHER

109   **JOB**

139   PSALMS

So the
king sought
advice.

1 Kings

GENRE: *Historical Narrative*

AUTHOR / DATE WRITTEN

Jeremiah • c. 960–850 BC

MAJOR THEMES — *Building of the Temple, Division of the Kingdom, Conflicting Worship of Gods*

KEY WORDS — *Temple, Covenant Faithfulness, Kingship*

KEY VERSE

1 KINGS 12:28

So the king sought advice. Then he made two golden calves, and he said to the people, "Going to Jerusalem is too difficult for you. Israel, here are your gods who brought you up from the land of Egypt."

1 Kings 1–3

David's life, full of the highest highs and the lowest lows, is now drawing to a close. The first chapter of 1 Kings is particularly concerned with the king-ship—from the current king, David, to the false king, Adonijah, to the king who would be anointed, Solomon. With David's health declining, his son, Adonijah, sought to install himself as king in place of Solomon, who God chose to rule. Chapter 1 describes his attempted coup and how Solomon was finally anointed as the king over Israel.

David's death and his final instructions to Solomon are recorded in chapter 2. The shepherd king of Israel was just a man, but his life points to the Son of David, who would reign on David's throne forever (2 Samuel 7). David's instructions to Solomon are first a call for David to keep the covenant and follow the Lord—a charge to obey and walk in obedience to all that the Lord commanded. But even David's instructions remind us that David was only a man. There are some things David commands that we are unsure how to interpret. Was David acting justly for the kingdom, or was he seeking revenge on his enemies? It was likely some of both. Like all other humans, David was a man with mixed motives.

Chapter 3 introduces us to Solomon's wisdom. Solomon's request for wisdom is rooted in God's covenant promises. And his display of wisdom at the end of chapter 3 is a reminder of God's care for justice and those on the fringes of society. Yet, from the beginning of Solomon's reign, there are warning signs that he is not doing what he is supposed to do. His desire for wealth, women, political alliances, and worship in the high places points us to the sad reality that Solomon's heart was divided.

But Solomon also points us to Jesus, for it is Jesus who is the embodiment of true wisdom. It is Christ alone who can perfectly keep the covenant in our place. He is the true King who will reign forever. He is the faithful one, despite the unfaithfulness of man.

"It is Christ alone who can perfectly keep the covenant in our place."

Take a moment to reflect on the life and death of King David. Why was his impact so great? How does reflecting on his life, death, and future bloodline, which includes the birth of Jesus Christ, grow your understanding of God and His plans?

Despite the good things that we see of Solomon, what warning signs do you see in today's chapters?

Read James 1:5. How does it comfort you to understand that God delights in wisdom and giving wisdom to us freely? Spend some time in faith-filled prayer, asking that God would grant you wisdom.

1 Kings 4-6

With King Solomon reigning over all of Israel, 1 Kings 4:20 tells us that Judah and Israel were "as numerous as the sand by the sea." This was the fulfillment of the promise made to Abraham many generations before in the Abrahamic covenant. Israel was now a strong and mighty nation in the land God had promised to them (Genesis 17). 1 Kings 4 gives us a picture of this thriving nation living in peace and security. Yet sadly, we are already beginning to see faults in the life of Solomon. Though he led with wisdom, he disregarded some of the Lord's covenant commands. In 1 Kings 4:26, we learn of his multitude of horses which was contrary to the Lord's command for kings not to amass horses (Deuteronomy 17:16).

In 1 Kings 5 and 6, Solomon begins building the temple—fulfillment of another one of God's promises found in 2 Samuel 7, where God promises David that his son will build a house for the Lord. And the building of the temple brought another promise, echoing with reminders of the tabernacle. God would dwell with His people (1 Kings 6:13). It has always been God's desire to dwell with His people. From Eden to the tabernacle and the temple, God was telling His people of His desire to dwell with them. In John 1:14, we learn that the Word became flesh and came to dwell among us. The dwelling place of God is fulfilled in Jesus, who humbled Himself and became a man to dwell among His people. And this promise points us forward to a still future fulfillment in the new heaven and new earth when there is no temple but where God dwells in the midst of His people without sin and suffering (Revelation 21). For now, as the people of God, we are being built up into a temple of God as the church (Ephesians 2:21-22), and we yearn for the day when we experience the fullness of this promise.

The kingdom of Solomon was impressive, but the kingdom of Christ will be glorious beyond comparison. The words to Solomon from the Lord in chapter 6 tell us the conditions of the covenant. But there is only One who could keep those covenant conditions, and it is Jesus who keeps the covenant in our place.

"The kingdom of Christ will be glorious beyond comparison."

Meditate on the promise to Abraham and Sarah in Genesis 17. How is this fulfilled in 1 Kings 4:20? How does this fulfillment grow your understanding of God's character? Does this fulfillment comfort you to trust in God's timing?

Reread 1 Kings 5:4. Solomon acknowledges that God is the one who granted rest and reprieve from war and misfortune. Do you find yourself fully trusting in God — that His sovereignty would provide rest and reprieve for you? Do you acknowledge God as the source of all that you have been provided?

In chapter 6, we read about the complexity and artistry of the temple. How does this expand your understanding of God's character and the intricacies of God's beauty?

1 Kings 7-9

He is a God of covenants. In these chapters, we see the construction of Solomon's palace and the final construction of the temple. With the construction completed, the ark of the covenant is brought into this glorious structure. The end of chapter 8 records for us how God's glory came and filled the new temple. The language is reminiscent of the end of the book of Exodus as God's glory filled the tabernacle. From the beginning of the story and the first pages of Genesis, God seeks to dwell with His people, and here in 1 Kings, we see that come to pass in a new way in Solomon's temple.

Chapter 8 also includes Solomon's beautiful prayer of praise to God and the dedication of the temple. This beautiful prayer focuses on God's covenant character—God had kept His promises. And when Solomon looked at this glorious temple, he saw promises kept that had been made long ago. The dedication of the temple also served as a covenant renewal ceremony as Solomon rehearsed some of the promised blessings and conditions for those blessings. At the start of chapter 9, we see the Lord appear to Solomon again and remind him personally of the covenant and the consequences of disobedience. There would be a great blessing for God's people if they obeyed the covenant. But the people were unable to keep it, and Solomon as their leader would be one of the first to turn from the Lord and the covenant.

These chapters remind us of God's covenant nature. He is a God who keeps His word and His promises. There are so many beautiful verses in this section speaking of how the Lord has fulfilled His promises and kept every word of His promise. Not one word failed then, and we know that His words never will. Yet, we can now look back and see that as glorious as the fulfillment of this promise was, it was just the beginning of what God was doing to fulfill that covenant with David. This temple was a house built by David's son, but the covenant also looked forward to a spiritual house built by David's true and better Son, Jesus. This temple of His body is being built up even now in God's church (Ephesians 2:21-22). Solomon knew that God had been faithful, but He could not see all of the ways that God's faithfulness would be worked out. This stands as a reminder for us that our God is ever more faithful than we realize.

"He is a God who keeps His word and His promises."

In chapter 8, we see Solomon blessing the Lord, dedicating the temple, and offering sacrifices. As you meditate on how Solomon spoke to the Lord and spoke to His people, what are some things we can learn from him?

In 1 Kings 9:1-9, we read a stern warning from the Lord about what would happen to His people if they chose to wander away from Him. What does this tell you about God's character? How does this spur you on to continue in holiness?

How do these chapters remind us that God keeps His promises? How can this encourage us in our own lives?

1 Kings 10-12

The Lord is concerned with our hearts and is not impressed by the prosperity of this world — this is the message that we are left with at the end of Solomon's life.

In chapter 10, we are introduced to the Queen of Sheba as she has traveled a far distance to learn of the wisdom and wealth of Solomon, and she blesses the Lord when she sees the blessing of God in Solomon's life. But unfortunately, the beautiful picture of blessing does not last long.

The first words of chapter 11 tell us of Solomon's love for foreign wives, idolatrous women who Solomon pursued in his lust and quest for political power. This description of Solomon near the end of his reign stands in stark contrast to the words of 1 Kings 3:3 that tell us Solomon loved the Lord. Solomon's heart was divided, and ultimately it would be the love of the things of this world that would cost him—personally and in the loss of his kingdom. His wives turned his heart from the Lord, and soon he worshiped their false gods, building altars to worship them. So the Lord raised up adversaries for Solomon. His kingdom would be taken from him and divided, but God in His mercy would not take the kingdom completely. Our God is faithful, and He would not break His covenant with David.

Solomon's death comes at the end of chapter 11, and by chapter 12, we see the kingdom divided. This division is from the Lord and part of His plan. He promised that this would happen if the nation's kings did not follow the Lord, and now we see the division unfolding. The chapter tragically ends with Jeroboam living in fear, causing him to turn from the Lord as well. Though the Lord promised him that he would rule ten of the tribes, he was fearful and set up golden calves for the people to worship, something that may sound all too familiar.

Our God kept His covenant, but the people failed to meet the conditions of the covenant. They could not live up to God's righteous standard, but there was One coming who would perfectly keep God's law in our place. Jesus is the answer to the mess that Solomon had made. He is the perfect King that neither Solomon nor David could ever be. And He is the answer to every covenant promise. It is in Him we find hope for divided hearts.

"Jesus is the answer to the mess that Solomon had made."

Solomon's heart easily turned from the Lord because of his love for earthly things. What does this tell you about the attraction of the world? What are some things that tend to fool you into thinking that this world offers you true satisfaction?

What does 1 Kings 11:1-8 tell you about the importance of surrounding yourself with godly people?

Reread 1 Kings 11:34. How can you be encouraged in your day-to-day life by the faithfulness of the Lord keeping His promises? How does this demonstrate grace and mercy?

1 Kings 13-15

Scripture now begins to detail the reigns of the many kings of Israel and Judah, and much like the time of the judges, many of the kings are characterized by the fact that they did what was right in their own eyes but did not follow the Lord's instruction.

We are reminded that when our selfish thoughts and desires rule us, the outcome is not good. Chapter 13 points us over and over to the Word of the Lord, and yet sadly, it also tells of those who ignored God's Word, even prophets who lied and manipulated the Word of God and other people. And as we read these accounts, we are left longing for a better king and prophet.

The Lord gave Jeroboam the kingdom of Israel. It was promised to him by the prophet's word, yet Jeroboam did not follow the Lord. In chapter 14, we see that his son is ill, and he sends his wife to the same prophet who had told him of the Lord's promise of the kingdom. He tells her to disguise herself, and though the text does not tell us why, we can assume that it is because Jeroboam was not following the Lord like he had been told to do. The prophet did not have good news, and Jeroboam's son died. His sin impacted everyone in sight.

Chapter 15 takes us back to Judah, and Abijam is introduced. Abijam was the son of Rehoboam and the great-grandson of David, but he did not walk in the Lord's ways or follow David's example. But 1 Kings 15:4 reminds us that despite the unfaithfulness of these kings, there is One who is faithful. God would be faithful to keep the lamp of the Davidic line burning. In Asa, we are finally introduced to a good king whose heart wholly followed the Lord. He got rid of the male cult prostitutes and cleaned out the idols. He was not perfect, and we see that the high places where priests made offerings to other gods were not removed during his reign, but His heart followed the Lord.

King after king lets us down. Even the best kings like David and Asa did not follow the Lord perfectly. But these chapters continue pointing to One who is better. They point to Jesus, who is the true and better King and prophet. They point us to the One who will sit on David's throne forever. They point to the reason that God patiently endured—He was bringing Jesus—the only true King and one who would be merciful and good.

"They point to Jesus, who is the true and better King and prophet."

Sin always impacts more than just ourselves. How do we see that in today's passage?

What does today's passage teach you about the character of God?

Reread 1 Kings 15:14. What do you think a heart that is "wholly devoted to the Lord" looks like?

1 Kings 16-18

The kings of Israel in the north all continued to be bad kings.

Chapter 16 lists out quite a few kings for us. Over and over again, we see that these are kings whose hearts were far from the Lord—kings who were seeking their own glory, worshiping idols, and turning from the truth. And yet, we also see that through it all, God was sovereignly working out His plan. He is not thrown off course by the wickedness of men but is sovereignly in control of every moment of history.

We are introduced to Elijah in chapter 17. We do not learn much about who he is, and neither do we receive a list of his accolades. Instead, we see that the Lord raised him up with a message and for a purpose. Though not explicitly stated in the text here, we learn in James 5:16-17 that Elijah prayed for the rain to cease. Throughout Elijah's story, we see him as a man of prayer who went to God humbly, seeking His will above all else. This chapter introduces the widow in the city of Zarephath. Though she is an unnamed Gentile woman, she is a woman who will experience the grace of the God of Israel through provision and in the raising of her son. She provides food for the prophet, and each morning that her oil and flour were present served as a reminder of God's faithfulness and grace to her.

Chapter 18 provides a stunning presentation of God's power. Elijah confronts Ahab with his wickedness, and the events that follow include a gathering of the prophets of Baal and Elijah on Mount Carmel. The people are presented with a choice—to serve Baal or Yahweh. The prophets of Baal cry out to their false god to rain down fire from heaven to consume their offering, but nothing happens. Elijah even mocks them, "Maybe he's thinking it over; maybe he has wandered away; or maybe he's on the road. Perhaps he's sleeping and will wake up" (1 Kings 18:27). Though they try with all their might, their god was silent. Then Elijah steps up. Asking for water to be poured on the altar, making it even harder for the fire to consume anything, he prays a short but powerful prayer to the one true God. In an instant, fire came down from heaven, consuming not just the offering but the stones, the dust, and the water. Here God shows that He is the only God, and the people turn away from Baal. Then Elijah prays, and the Lord sent the rain.

"We must serve Him with everything we are because of who He is."

As great as these stories of Elijah are, we place our hope in One who is greater than Elijah. The stories point us to Jesus, who not only raised people from the dead and was Himself raised from the grave but has the power to raise us from the dead as well. Just as the people on Mount Carmel, our theology demands a response. If what God has said in His Word is true (and it is), we must serve Him with everything we are because of who He is.

QUESTIONS

How does Elijah's story strengthen your faith?

What does this passage teach you about prayer?

Think about the choices that Elijah gave in 1 Kings 18:21. The way of Baal led to death, but the way of the Lord leads to life. It seems like a clear choice, but what are some ways you find yourself in the habit of choosing false idols, whatever they may be for you?

1 Kings 19-22

After such a mighty victory in chapter 18, chapter 19 begins with Ahab telling Jezebel what Elijah has done.

Elijah must now run for his life right after a major victory. He feels alone and discouraged, and it is then that the Lord speaks to Elijah in a low whisper. Though He holds all power in heaven and earth, God speaks with a gentle voice to His child. Elijah was a prophet in a time that men and kings rejected the Lord, and yet he was faithful even when he was alone. Though it seemed that everyone was against him, Elijah knew that God was for him. The Lord promised to leave a remnant of 7,000 people who would serve the Lord and not follow Baal, and God would keep that promise.

These chapters continue with a war between Israel and Syria and Ahab and Ben-hadad. Though Ahab had victory just as the prophet had promised, he did evil in the sight of the Lord by releasing the evil Ben-hadad. Ahab's sin seems to compound when Ahab covets the vineyard of a man named Naboth. Ahab wanted what was not his, and corrupted by his power, he colludes with his wife, Jezebel, to take what he wants through deceit, manipulation, and eventually murder. But the Lord is not caught off guard by Ahab and Jezebel's deceit. Ahab is condemned and finally repents.

However, the final chapter of 1 Kings implies that Ahab's repentance was not genuine. The chapter presents false prophets and their false prophecy as well as Micaiah, who is a prophet from the Lord (and perhaps the same prophet from chapter 20). Micaiah's prophecy condemns Ahab for how he left the people of Israel like sheep without a shepherd. And the final page of 1 Kings ends with Ahab getting killed in battle, Jehosophat reigning in Judah, and Ahaziah reigning in Israel.

In our lives, there will be times when we feel that we are the only ones standing for the Lord. But even when we feel completely alone, we can know that He is always with us. He is there, calling us by name and speaking with a still small voice. These chapters point us to Jesus, the Good Shepherd who Ahab could never be. He is the Shepherd who gently leads and loves His own without ever abusing His power.

"Even when we feel completely alone, we can know that He is always with us."

1 Kings 19:7-8 describes an angel telling Elijah that the journey on which the Lord is sending him is too great for him, and the angel tells him to eat the food in front of him. For forty days, Elijah journeys on the strength of this food provided to him by the angel. How does this grow your understanding that the Lord is our supplier of strength?

What is the significance of God's voice coming through a whisper rather than through a fire, earthquake, or strong wind?

Read John 10:1-18. Contrast Jesus with Ahab.

since
he had
promised

2 Kings

GENRE: *Historical Narrative*

AUTHOR / DATE WRITTEN
Jeremiah • c. 850–560 BC

MAJOR THEMES — *Covenant Kingship, Exile from the Promised Land, Rebellion Against God*

KEY WORDS — *Exile, Judgment, Idol Worship, Prophets*

KEY VERSE

2 KINGS 8:19

For the sake of his servant David, the Lord was unwilling to destroy Judah, since he had promised to give a lamp to David and his sons forever.

2 Kings 1-3

2 Kings opens shortly after the death of the evil king, Ahab.

Ahaziah is reigning over Israel, and the text informs us of his injury and subsequent inquisition to Baal-zebub. Instead of turning to the Lord in his distress, Ahaziah went to a false god, and Elijah quickly confronted him for seeking hope apart from the Lord. Elijah prophesies that Ahaziah will die, and that prophecy quickly comes true. Elijah pleaded for evil men to return to the Lord and rest in His covenant faithfulness, but time and time again, these evil kings would choose the judgment of the Lord over His promises of mercy.

In chapter 2, Elijah is taken to heaven on a chariot of fire. There is no mention of death in Elijah's story, and Elisha watches as his predecessor is called up to heaven. Elisha enters the scene as Elijah's replacement. This is displayed as Elisha asks, "Where is the Lord God of Elijah?" And as the waters part before Him, it is clear that God is with Elisha, and he steps into his role as prophet.

Chapter 3 introduces us to Jehoram, the son of Ahab, who is now king over Israel, and to Jehosophat, the king of Judah. Jehoram was an evil king like his father, but Jehosophat was a good, though imperfect, king. Elisha proclaimed the Word of the Lord to these kings as they fought together against Moab, and the Lord showed mercy because Jehosophat followed the Lord.

These passages point us to our need and desire for a better king. Even good kings like Jehosophat were riddled with flaws and sinful choices. Jehosophat was a good king, but He was not the King we long for. Jesus is that King. Elijah prophesied of the judgment of God for sin, but Jesus is the true and better prophet who bore the judgment of God in our place. Elisha, through God's power, parted the waters before him, and Jesus, by His own power, would still the raging storms. Elisha spoke the Word of God, and Jesus is the Word made flesh (John 1:14). There is only one prophet who can redeem, and that is Jesus, who is our hope and our Redeemer. These passages make us long for a true and better king and prophet, which we only find in Jesus.

"There is only one prophet who can redeem, and that is Jesus, who is our hope and our Redeemer."

Spend some time in reflection over the differences between Ahaziah and Elijah. What is the most striking difference to you? How can your walk with God grow as a result of reading about the lives of these two men?

Reread 2 Kings 2:9. How does this verse remind you of when Solomon asked for wisdom? What can we learn about what is valuable and what should be prioritized from these men's requests?

How do these chapters point you to Christ?

2 Kings 4-6

During this turbulent time in the history of Israel, God was still at work.

People were placing their faith in Yahweh (the Hebrew name for God), and God was still working great miracles through the prophets. We begin to see many short accounts of what God was doing and what was happening in the land, and through it all, we can see God's faithful hand at work. God was not absent, and we can be assured He is not absent now.

Chapter 4 shows us Elisha performing miracles, proclaiming the truth, and having compassion for those in need. From providing an abundance of oil for a poor widow to providing a son for a barren woman, God is a God who provides. This chapter shows us the love and compassion of God in raising the Shunammite woman's son from the dead. Despite the great sin and difficulty of this time in Israel's history, God was still at work, and He was calling out a faithful remnant of people to love and serve Him.

In the story of Naaman, we learn of a man who was healed of His leprosy at the urging of a young servant girl. God does not always work the way that we would expect, but He is always faithful. In this account, we see an enemy ruler being healed and placing faith in Yahweh. Yet, we also see the Israelite Gehazi being afflicted with leprosy due to his greed and deceit. God calls His own from every nation, and even here in Israel's history, we can see the grafting in of those once far from God. God called Naaman to Himself, even though Naaman was from an enemy nation. This is how God works. He pursues His own and offers healing and hope amid a world of uncertainty.

God cares about the details. Whether to widows, older women, young servant girls, men dealing with disease, or to you and me, He will be faithful to his people. The final chapter of today's passage points us to God's grace and mercy in even providing for His enemies. What a beautiful picture of the gospel that paints for the children of God who were once His enemies. Elisha points us to Jesus. Jesus is the ultimate picture of one who heals, loves, and has compassion on all those He meets. It is Jesus who runs to the outsider, and it is Jesus who extends mercy and grace to those who were once enemies of God. Jesus is the one who meets our needs and provides more than we could ever ask or imagine.

"God cares about the details."

How can you be comforted in the fact that God defied the laws of physics to provide more oil for the widow? How does this give you confidence in His willingness and ability to provide for you?

How does Elisha point us to Jesus?

What stands out most to you in these chapters? In what way?

2 Kings 7-9

God is faithful. He always keeps His promises.

He always does what He says that He will do. This theme seems to ring out again and again in these historical books. The prophet Elisha boldly proclaimed that the famine would end. However, after years of famine, his words seemed nearly impossible. But Elisha spoke the word of the Lord, and the very next day, just as Elisha had said, the famine ended. Every word of Elisha's prophecy had come true. God was faithful to provide and faithful to His word.

Chapter 8 continues with the reminder that the Lord cares for His own. The same Shunammite woman who was introduced in chapter 4 is back, and this time, God's faithfulness to her is again on display. During the time of famine, though she and her family fled in obedience to Elisha's instructions, they came back at the end of the famine, and the king restored everything that belonged to them and more. God provides for His people, and He is faithful each step of the way.

Over and over again, we see the evil kings who would reign over Israel and Judah. Kings are murdered, and new kings are anointed to reign. At the end of chapter 9, we see the demise of the evil Jezebel. Although it would be so easy to question whether God had forgotten His promises made so long before, we are given a sweet reminder in 2 Kings 8:19. Despite the wickedness of the kings who came after him, God did not destroy Judah for David's sake. God would be faithful to His covenant. God made a promise, and He would keep it. This is the promise of the One who would come from David's line. It is a promise of Jesus. God would be faithful to His people by sending Jesus—the answer to the sin, the suffering, and the mess found in the pages of these historical books and the hearts of humanity.

Over and over again, we see the magnificent faithfulness of God. Even when we stray, He is faithful. His love for His people has never wavered. He is sure and steadfast. It is His great love that compels us to serve Him with our lives and rest in confident assurance that as He has always been faithful, He will continue to be faithful to us.

"God made a promise, and He would keep it."

What can we learn from Elisha's great faith in chapter 7? What do we learn about God's character in this chapter?

Reread 2 Kings 8:19. How does God's steadfastness to keep His promises comfort you? How does this act of God strengthen your understanding of the permanence of covenants?

In 2 Kings 9:6-10, we read a promise from God about what will become of Jezebel, and later in the chapter, we see this promise fulfilled. How does this expand your understanding of God's sovereignty? Do you believe that God's plans cannot be thwarted?

2 Kings 10-12

Jehu's story continues in chapter 10. We can see that he was a cunning king who worked to rid the nation of Ahab's descendants as well as the prophets of Baal.

We can appreciate Jehu's desire to remove the evil and idolatrous influences. Unfortunately, we also later see that Jehu did not tear down the high places where priests made offerings to false gods and continued in the sins of Jeroboam. 2 Kings 10:31 tells us that he "was not careful to follow the instruction of the Lord God of Israel with all his heart." Sadly, this was true of so many of the kings and is a sober admonition to us as well.

In 2 Kings 11:1-3, we are introduced to a young woman named Jehosheba. Though she is largely unknown, she plays a massive part in the story of Scripture. The evil Athaliah, who was the mother of Ahaziah, set out to kill all of the line of David and make herself ruler, but Jehosheba took Joash, her young nephew, and hid him in the temple for six years. He was hidden away until the time was right for him to become king. During his kingship, he did what was right in the eyes of the Lord under the instruction of the high priest.

It may seem like an odd and insignificant story, but we must remember that this is the line through which Jesus was promised to come. God in His sovereignty would not allow the Davidic line to be destroyed. He would use a young woman determined to live courageously to save the line of the Messiah. God keeps His promises. He does not neglect His covenant. He is faithful to His word.

The Lord is sovereign over all, and He will bring His plan to pass, but He also delights to use His children. The Lord magnificently used Jehosheba. Though she is not well known and many people have never even heard her name, her act of sacrifice and bravery had a great impact. God used her to preserve the line of David, which was ultimately the line of Jesus. He alone would be the one to keep every promise of the covenants. And He would be the one to be the true and better King that even the best kings of Israel could never be.

"He is faithful to His word."

In 2 Kings 10:1-17, we read that Jehu wiped out the relatives and descendants of Ahab. How does this contrast to what is seen in 2 Kings 11:1-3 in the preservation of David's line? How does this inform your belief in God's sovereignty?

Reread 2 Kings 10:31. We see here that Jehu's carelessness to walk fully with the Lord led the whole of Israel to sin. What does this tell you about the importance of walking in the Lord with your whole heart?

In 2 Kings 12:2, it is revealed that Jehoash did what was right in God's sight because the priest, Jehoiada, instructed him. How does this grow your perception of the importance of teaching and discipleship?

2 Kings 13-15

Our God is a covenant-keeping God. He is faithful to His Word and always keeps His promises.

These historical narratives point us toward His steadfast love for His people, even when they are living sinful lives. He is always seeking to bring them back to Himself. In chapters 13-15, He hears and sees their afflictions and comes to their rescue even though they were not serving Him with their whole hearts (2 Kings 13:4-5, 13:23, 14:26-27).

These chapters recount for us king after king in Israel and Judah. Some were certainly better than others, but each was riddled with problems. Chapter 13 begins with Jehoahaz in Israel. The text says that he did what was evil in the sight of the Lord, yet he sought the favor of the Lord. It seems that he wanted God's blessing without having to obey Him. And yet, God is merciful. The text says that God gave Israel a savior or deliverer. This person is never named but would have been someone who helped them through the battle. Ultimately, however, it was the Lord who was caring for and delivering His people. Nevertheless, the people did not repent.

Many kings would rise and fall, and king after king would do evil. Occasionally, one of the southern kings is described as doing what was right in the eyes of the Lord. But even the very best kings could not permanently take away the high places of idol worship, for each time a king removed the high places, the people would eventually resurrect new gods and altars in their place.

2 Kings 13:23 tells us that the Lord was gracious and compassionate to His people. Despite all the evil they allowed to penetrate the nation, He still extended grace. In fact, this verse says that He turned toward them. After all they had done, He still pursued them in love and remembered the promise that He had made. God promised through His covenant to Abraham, Isaac, Jacob, and David, and God would be faithful. The ultimate display of this faithfulness would come by God sending the one true Savior and deliverer in Jesus Christ who would rescue and redeem His own. Our God pursues us. He turns toward us. We have never sinned too much that He does not stand waiting to redeem. The story of redemption is this—that while we rejected Him and ran to sin, in love, He ran to us (Romans 5:8).

"Despite all the evil they allowed to penetrate the nation, He still extended grace."

Meditate on the grace exemplified in 2 Kings 13:23. Spend some time in self-reflection about a time that God extended grace to you when you were undeserving. How do these instances grow your faith and trust in the Lord?

2 Kings 15:35 tells us that though Jotham did what was right in the eyes of the Lord, "Yet the high places were not taken down." This has been a pattern in each king's reign that we have seen so far. What does this tell you about the grip that sin can have on a person? Spend some time in prayer, asking that God would reveal your sin to you and give you the strength to obey Him.

With the number of kings we have seen so far, we have seen that each of them has only partially obeyed the Lord. Yet, God has been long-suffering with Israel despite this. What does this tell you about God's patience and grace toward us?

2 Kings 16-18

In 2 Kings 16, we are introduced to Ahaz. Ahaz's name is definitely on the list of evil kings.

This evil king in Judah did not do what was right in God's eyes. Ahaz even introduced child sacrifice to Judah, sacrificing his son as an offering to a false god. His sin would bring great consequences and military defeat.

Things were bad in Judah and even worse in Israel. In chapter 17, we watch the downfall of the northern kingdom of Israel. After all that the Lord had done for them, they continued to rebel and run after other gods, and now they would face exile from their homeland as a result of their idolatry and rebellion. In His great love and mercy, God sent prophet after prophet to warn them, but they would not listen. The children of Israel were stubborn, did not listen to God's Word, ran after false gods, and followed the nations. This chapter provides a pivotal turning point in Israel's history as they are carried away into exile in Assyria. The end of chapter 17 reminds us of the beautiful covenant that God made with His people, and then verse 40 simply tells us that they would not listen. They wanted to do things their own way. They embraced their own version of syncretism, which is when religions are mixed. They wanted to say that they feared the Lord, but they would not give up their idols. The results for Israel were tragic.

Chapter 18 gives us a glimpse into the life of Hezekiah, a king of Judah who followed the Lord. Hezekiah is one of the best kings that Judah ever had, and he is even compared to King David. He did what was right in the eyes of God, and finally, he tore down the high places that had been built for false gods. He also destroyed the bronze serpent of Moses that the people had begun to worship. Determined to restore right worship in Judah, he worked hard to do so. Under Hezekiah's rule, the temple and sacrificial system were restored, and the people once again began celebrating the feasts and festivals, such as the Passover, that God had commanded them to keep. So while things seemed to be falling apart in Israel, God's people in Judah were repenting and turning to the Lord once again.

Hezekiah was a good king, and after a line of so many bad kings, it is a breath of fresh air to see what he did in Judah. Hezekiah grows our longing for a better king, King Jesus. He is the one who is gracious and merciful to His people. Despite our stubbornness and rebellion, God never stops pursuing His own.

"Despite our stubbornness and rebellion, God never stops pursuing His own."

Chapter 17 is a pivotal point in Israel's history where we read that Israel is exiled because they have so greatly sinned. Read 2 Kings 17:17-18. What does this tell you about how deeply we can be involved with sin when we are only partially obeying the Lord?

In 2 Kings 17:7-8, before the author explains what becomes of Israel, he first points out the many things that God has done for Israel. Why do you think the author emphasizes this?

Reread 2 Kings 18:3-8. Judah finally has a godly king! Meditate on the importance of this, and further examine verses 6 and 7. What are the ways you hold fast to the Lord?

2 Kings 19-21

Hezekiah came into the scene as a refreshing reminder of a king who loves the Lord and seeks to serve Him.

But, he was not a perfect king. Hezekiah ruled over Judah in this time when men did not follow the Lord, and yet we see him stand up for truth and trust in the Lord. We can see an example of Hezekiah's trust in the Lord in his prayer in chapter 19. This prayer was prayed amid national conflict when Sennacherib questioned the power of God to save His people. The Lord promised to defend the city, and verse 34 tells us that He would do it for His own sake and David's sake. God would be faithful to the covenant promises that He had made to His people. He would not forget His promises, and His Word would come to pass.

In chapter 20, the Lord hears the prayers of Hezekiah as he is about to die, and the Lord adds fifteen years to his life. But Hezekiah was not a perfect king; his pride leads to his downfall in his later years. It seems that all the success and prosperity had gone to his head, and he was more concerned about his own reign than for the future of the nation.

After Hezekiah's death, we see his sons and grandsons reign after him. And sadly, his offspring did not share the same good qualities that Hezekiah had. His son, Manasseh, was a wicked king. He did what was evil in the sight of the Lord, and the text even points out how he set up pagan altars in the center of the temple and even burned his own son as an offering to a false god. His sin would have dire consequences for the people of God. His rule was followed by his son, Amon, who was another bad king. He also did what was evil in the sight of the Lord and abandoned the God of His people.

These chapters show us a good king who was overcome by his pride, as well as some very bad kings. However, the greatest and most evil kings cannot thwart God's good plans. The plan of God was determined before the world was even formed (2 Kings 19:25). And that glorious plan of redemption points us to a better king—a king who would not rule with pride but with humility. This king would not oppress but comfort. This king is Jesus, and our text today makes us long for His kingdom and His reign. From these chapters, we can learn to be faithful to our King, to come to Him in prayer, and to always trust His plan, knowing that He will always do what He has promised.

"The greatest and most evil kings cannot thwart God's good plans."

Think about the comfort Hezekiah must have experienced when the Lord heard his prayer. Do you find yourself praying with full confidence that the Lord hears you?

In chapter 20, the Lord once again proves that He hears the cries of His people. Read Psalm 18:30. Are you comforted in the fact that God hears our cries and does what is best for us? Spend some time in prayer, asking God that He would make your desires align with what is good for you in His sight.

How do the kings in these chapters leave us longing for Jesus?

2 Kings 22-25

The close of 2 Kings provides a reminder of all we have seen in the books of 1 and 2 Kings.

In just a few chapters, we see the highest highs and the lowest lows of the divided kingdom. The reign of Josiah stands out as one of the best times for Judah. He is a king who followed the Lord with all of his heart and soul.

Early in Josiah's reign—after he commanded the temple be repaired—the book of the law was found after being neglected for some time. The priests went to the prophetess Huldah for instruction, and she shared a message from the Lord. These words of God brought the king to repentance, and the repentance that took place was both personal and corporate. The words of God were the foundation of Josiah's reign as king, and under Josiah's leadership, the people followed the Lord. During his reign, Josiah repaired the temple and restored worship. And, like Hezekiah, he tore down the high places and altars of false gods and reinstated the celebration of Passover. Scripture tells us that there was no king like him. His love for the Lord and his leadership of God's people brought revival in the hearts of God's people and impacted the entire culture of Judah at the time.

Unfortunately, it seems that the revival was too late, and the kings who followed him quickly returned to doing what was evil in the sight of the Lord. Jehoahaz, Jehoiakim, Jehoiachin, and Zedekiah did what was evil in God's eyes and returned Judah to the sad days before Josiah's reign. Unfortunately, the fall, captivity, and exile of Judah would soon follow. And yet, even as Jerusalem was captured and the Israelites are exiled from their home, we are reminded of God's grace. The people were facing the judgment they had caused by turning from the Lord, yet even in exile, the Lord would be with them. He would not leave them or abandon His promises.

Josiah was a good king who seemed to bring hope and restoration to the people of Judah. There was no king better than him—at least not an earthly king. As the true King of Judah, Jesus would be a true and better king for the people of God. He leads His people with love and grace and is the answer to every covenant promise of God. God would graciously preserve the line of Judah to bring forth the Lion of the Tribe of Judah to rescue and redeem His own. Along the way, He was faithful to be with His people, whether at home or in exile, and we can be confident that He will not leave us.

"He leads His people with love and grace and is the answer to every covenant promise of God."

At the close of chapter 21, we see two more evil kings of Judah who abandoned the ways of the Lord. But as chapter 22 begins, we see that Josiah, at the age of eight years old, did what was right in the Lord's sight. What does this tell you about age and our capability to obey God?

Reread 2 Kings 23:25, and then read Deuteronomy 6:5. What do these two verses reveal about what the Lord most desires from us?

We have now come to the end of 2 Kings. What are some of the most important things you have learned from reading this book? In what ways has your understanding of God grown?

Yours, Lord, is the kingdom.

1 Chronicles

GENRE: *Historical Narrative*

AUTHOR / DATE WRITTEN

Unknown, possibly Ezra • c. 450-425 BC

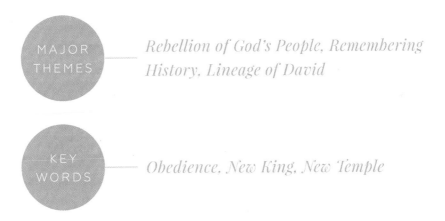

MAJOR THEMES — *Rebellion of God's People, Remembering History, Lineage of David*

KEY WORDS — *Obedience, New King, New Temple*

KEY VERSE

1 CHRONICLES 29:11

Yours, Lord, is the greatness and the power and the glory and the splendor and the majesty, for everything in the heavens and on earth belongs to you. Yours, Lord, is the kingdom, and you are exalted as head over all.

1 Chronicles 1-6

Interestingly, 1 and 2 Chronicles were originally one book that was divided due to scroll length, as books were originally stored on scrolls. Though many of the accounts recorded in the Chronicles overlap with other books in the Canon, they provide a new perspective. This book is situated at the very end of the Hebrew Bible, yet it is interesting to note the very first word of the first chapter is "Adam." The book of 1 Chronicles begins with chapters of genealogies to take the reader back to the first man. The author begins his story at the very beginning to show God's redemptive plan for His people.

There are perhaps very few people who name genealogies as their favorite genre of biblical writing. At first glance, these lists of names may feel monotonous and boring; however, when we realize that these lists of names chronicle the story of the people of God and layout the lineage of David from which the Messiah would come, we realize just how important these names are. Each name represents a person given a specific role in the story of redemption. God creates each person in His image and knows them by name.

These names would have been familiar to the original audience, who would have known Israel's history well. This was their family tree, full of all the good and the bad that family trees bring. If we are ever tempted to gloss over these lists of names, we must remember that, if we are God's children, this is our family tree as well. These are the people who went before us in God's story. We, too, have been given a role to play in this grand drama. Though at times we may feel that our role is insignificant, we have been placed right where we are by the Lord to bring Him glory. He calls us each by name, and only He knows all the details of how our own lives will intersect with this great story of redemption.

Though not recorded in the pages of Chronicles, these genealogies would be fulfilled generations after the last words would be written on the original scrolls. These genealogies find their fulfillment in the final name of another genealogy recorded for us in Matthew 1:16, where we are introduced to the promised Son of Israel, "Jesus who is called the Christ." These chapters tell His story, and as children of God, they tell our story as well.

"We have been placed right where we are by the Lord to bring Him glory."

While reading genealogies can be difficult, reflect on the ways reading through 1 and 2 Kings helped you understand some of the people behind the names mentioned in 1 Chronicles 1-6.

Meditate on 2 Timothy 3:16-17. Spend some time in prayer, asking that God would give you the wisdom, patience, and attitude needed to profit from your Bible reading.

Read Matthew 1:1-17, focusing on verse 17. How does this passage grow your understanding of the importance of genealogies?

1 Chronicles 7-9

The genealogies continue in chapters 7-9. Here, we are introduced to the genealogies of the tribe of Benjamin and specifically of Saul, the failed king of Israel.

It may seem a little confusing that chapter 7 is a genealogy of the tribe of Benjamin, and chapter 8 is as well, though it is different. The Chronicler first takes a zoomed-out look at the tribe of Benjamin and its mighty men and then zooms in to give us the backstory on a very significant character in Israel's story. Chapter 8 examines the history of Saul, who was the first king of Israel. The Chronicler uses the genealogies to set the stage and the main characters for the history that he is about to retell.

In chapter 9, the author flashes forward many years ahead and lists genealogies of those who would return first after the exile. The author also takes time to mention those who worked and served in the temple in a variety of roles. The text tells us that the Lord was with these servants of Yahweh. Their work was an important part of what God was doing in His people, and we will learn more about their service soon. We know from our reading of 1 and 2 Kings that the story ahead holds much rebellion from the people of Israel. Yet, it also holds so many reminders of the Lord's mercy and grace toward His people.

The location of these genealogies is a little flicker of the hope that lies ahead. The people would rebel, and yet through it all, the Lord would be ever faithful. He would be patiently waiting, ready to bring them home. Most importantly, it would be through the line of David that God would send the promised King. Jesus would come to be the King, but He would also come to serve. He would humble Himself to redeem.

God would be faithful to His people. Despite rebellion and exile, the Lord was not far off. He rescues and redeems. He is patient and merciful. And, He allows them to sense their desperate need for Him. Our God does the same with us. He is ever patient, ever-merciful, and ever-loving. He pleads with us to return and offers hope, redemption, and restoration through Jesus.

"Despite rebellion and exile, the Lord was not far off."

What are some ways that you see God working through the genealogies in chapters 7-9?

How can reading through genealogies grow your understanding of how faithful the Lord is? Do these chapters grow your confidence in God's plan?

Through these chapters, we are reminded of Israel's rebellion. How does being reminded of their disobedience also remind you of God's grace, mercy, and steadfastness?

1 Chronicles 10-12

In these chapters, the author moves away from genealogies and introduces readers to Saul and David.

The contrast between these two kings is great. In the retelling of Saul's death, the reader is reminded that he was not faithful to the Lord in his life. His lack of faithfulness was the reason for his death and rejection from the throne. The text explicitly states that it was the Lord who put Saul to death (1 Chronicles 10:14) and gave the throne and kingdom to David. In contrast to Saul, David was a man after God's own heart (Acts 13:22). Though David would make many mistakes, his heart would always return to the Lord. The journey to kingship was not an easy one for David. This anointing came fifteen years after David was anointed king by Samuel. Yet, through the waiting, God's purposes for David never changed, and God would be faithful to fulfill every word of His promises to David.

God's presence with David is seen from the start of his kingship. 1 Chronicles 11:9 points out that David became greater and greater because the Lord was with him. David would be the shepherd of Israel, and the Lord would be with Him as He led the people of Israel. When the inhabitants of Jerusalem refused to allow David to come to the city that God promised, the Lord had other plans. David was victorious in taking the land that God promised Him.

We are introduced to David's mighty men in chapters 11-12, but again we are reminded in 1 Chronicles 11:14 that though the men were great, it was the Lord who gave the victory. Like David and his mighty men, the same is true for us—our successes and victories are always dependent on the Lord. We can rest in that truth and know that His ways are higher, and His plan is perfect (2 Samuel 22:31, Psalm 18:30). We can simply serve the Lord and leave the victory in His faithful hands.

David was a king chosen from among the people (Psalm 89:19). Yet, there would be another king and descendant of Judah who would fulfill every promise made to David. Jesus was the chosen one who came from God—God made flesh. He came from the people so that He might redeem His people. And all victory comes from Him, for Him, through Him, and to Him.

"Jesus was the chosen one who came from God—God made flesh."

Meditate on the differences between Saul and David. How does each man's life underscore the importance of being faithful to the Lord?

1 Chronicles 11:10 describes the mighty men as individuals who gave David "strong support." What does this tell us about the importance of friendships within the church? Are you offering ministerial support to those who are around you? In what way?

Reflect on 2 Samuel 22:31 and Psalm 18:30. Spend some time in prayer, thanking God that He alone brings victory.

1 Chronicles 13-15

This was a significant step as the nation sought to return to the Lord under David's reign. The plan to bring back the ark was a good one. Unfortunately, David and the people did not follow the clear instructions that God had given them for how to transport the ark. God is holy, and He had given a specific plan for how the ark was to be transported. Instead of moving the ark in the manner that God had prescribed, they did it their way. Perhaps it seemed easier, or perhaps they were simply careless and did not consult God's instructions. Whatever the case may be, the consequences were dire. Uzzah dies when he reaches out and touches the ark to keep it from falling. God is concerned about things being done His way. It seems that David momentarily abandoned the plan to move the ark, and it was left in the house of Obed-edom. The Lord blessed the household of Obed-edom during those three months that the ark was present there.

Meanwhile, David was in Jerusalem. The Lord had established him as king of Israel, and God's favor was obvious in his life. But chapter 14 hints at some problematic aspects of David's life as well. The text tells us that he was multiplying wives and wealth. Yet, it also tells us that David inquired of the Lord for wisdom in battle and leadership. It seems that David had more wisdom in his professional life than in his personal life. This would be a recurring theme throughout his life.

In chapter 15, David resumes his mission to bring the ark to Jerusalem, and this time it would be done the right way. David confessed that they had not originally followed the Lord's instruction, but he committed to following the Lord's commands this time.

These chapters remind us that God is holy and righteous. He gives commands for a reason, even when we do not understand the reason. David was an imperfect king, and this only reminds us that Jesus is the true and better King who follows God's law perfectly in our place. He is perfect in all of His ways, and we can trust that His commands for us are good.

"He is perfect in all of His ways, and we can trust that His commands for us are good."

The ark was being transported improperly, which is why it became unstable, and Uzzah felt the need to steady it. What does this tell you about the importance of listening to God and fully obeying His commands? Does this also give you insight into trusting God's purposes, even if they do not seem to make practical sense?

Reread 1 Chronicles 14:15. How does this verse strengthen your confidence in God and grow your understanding of His character?

Think about the picture of worship that is given in 1 Chronicles 15:16-28. How does this passage grow your understanding of the purpose of worship? Does this passage change your perception regarding how we should all participate in worship?

1 Chronicles 16-18

With the ark finally in its tent in Jerusalem, David is full of thankfulness to the Lord, as evident in the song of thankfulness and praise recorded in 1 Chronicles 16.

David is overwhelmed with gratitude for all that the Lord has done, and this psalm is a sweet example of what the attitude of our hearts should be. Many of the words of this song may seem very familiar if you have read the Psalms. This song is a compilation of many of the psalms giving praise to the Lord. David gives several commands of action that are just as applicable to us today as they were to the original audience. This song is a retelling of the story of Israel's history. From the calling of Abraham to God's covenant with His people, this song highlights how God has been working in every step of Israel's journey. God never left their side; even when they did not know what He was doing, He was there.

In chapter 17, the author points his readers to one of the most pivotal moments in Scripture. These events are also recorded in 2 Samuel 7, and they are known as the Davidic Covenant. With the ark in Jerusalem, David desired to build a house for the Lord so that God's house was not a tent when the king lived in a palace. David even mentioned this desire to the prophet Nathan, who also thought it sounded like a great idea. But the Lord came to Nathan that night with instructions that David was not to build a house for the Lord. But it is what the Lord said next that is so shocking. God did not want David to build Him a house; instead, He would build a house for David. However, the house that God was speaking of was not made of wood or stone. God would build David a dynasty, a kingdom, and a family. And someday, a ruler would sit on David's throne whose kingdom and reign would last forever. God was promising to send the greatest King the world would ever know. He was promising to send the Messiah whose kingdom would have no end—this is called the Davidic covenant. The Davidic covenant was a promise of Jesus.

David's response was humble gratitude, and the following chapter shows how the Lord was with David in everything that he did. As David administered

"We should seek Him and remember all that He has done."

justice and equity, God was with Him. God was the one who gave every victory, and He is the one who would keep every promise.

These verses remind us of how we should come before the Lord and let our lives overflow with praise each day. We should seek Him and remember all that He has done. We should ascribe Him all the glory He deserves and worship Him for who He is, resting in His faithfulness each day of our lives.

QUESTIONS

Meditate on David's song of thanks in chapter 16. What are some things that stick out to you the most about this song? How do these things strengthen your relationship with the Lord?

Reread 1 Chronicles 17:18-19. Notice here that David refers to himself as a servant of God. What does this tell you about the posture we should take when we pray? What does this tell you about our identity in Christ?

In 1 Chronicles 18:13, we read that the Lord gave victory to David wherever he went. Why did the Lord do this? What can we learn from David because of this?

1 Chronicles 19–21

Chapter 19 opens with the story of the Ammonites disgracing David's men.

David wanted to be kind to Hanun after his father's death, but the Ammonites were skeptical of David's kindness and did not trust him. The Ammonites shamed David's men and incited war. Joab led the army of Israel and encouraged them to use their strength for the glory of God and to trust the Lord to do what was best.

Chapter 20 begins with an interesting reminder about the time that kings go out to war. Though not mentioned in the text of 1 Chronicles, this is the time when David's sin with Bathsheba took place. You can read that account in 2 Samuel 11-12. David neglected to be where he should have been, which resulted in sin.

On the heels of David's great worship and military victories come descriptions of some of David's greatest sins. In Chapter 21, David takes a census of the people. Though taking a census was not forbidden, Scripture makes it clear that this was wrong as it was Satan standing against Israel. Though the census was usually taken to gather the tax, this census was likely based on pride over all that the nation had accomplished. We know that David's heart was not in the right place by his reaction when confronted. He knew that he had sinned greatly.

When the Lord sent pestilence as punishment for the sin, David built an altar to sacrifice to the Lord. David refused to take the land for free, as he would not offer to the Lord something that cost him nothing. This land was the same place Abraham had been willing to sacrifice Isaac (Genesis 22) and the place that the temple would be built. God used David's greatest failures to bring about His plan. The temple would be built by Solomon, the son of Bathsheba. God would redeem David's sin for His glory.

God showed great grace to David, and He shows great grace to us as well. This is most evidenced in the promised Son who would come through David's line. We see a glimpse of the Son of God in these chapters when the text describes the angel of the Lord whose judgment was withheld because of a sacrifice for

"God showed great grace to David, and He shows great grace to us as well."

sin. This is exactly what God does for us through Jesus. Though our sin is great, judgment is withheld for those who place their trust in the finished sacrifice of Jesus. We can trust the Lord to do what is right, and even in our sin and weakness, we can trust in the grace and mercy of our faithful King.

QUESTIONS

Reread 1 Chronicles 19:13. Do you trust that the Lord is doing what He sees as good? Do you have confidence in His sovereign plan?

In 1 Chronicles 21:15-26, we see God extend mercy on David and His people. How does this passage grow your understanding of God's character?

Reflect on 1 Chronicles 21:24. What does it look like in our modern lives not to give to God what costs us nothing?

1 Chronicles 22-25

Right after David's great sin and sacrifice on Mount Moriah, he began to prepare for the building of the temple by his son, Solomon.

The temple would be built at the very spot that David had sacrificed to the Lord. It must have been a reminder to David that he had been forgiven and restored. Scholars have suggested that this may have been the time that David wrote Psalm 30. It is a psalm of praise for the dedication of the temple, and the words are powerful when we are reminded of all that the Lord had done for David. After making preparations for the temple and purchasing the land, David told Solomon about the covenant promises of God and the command of the Lord that Solomon would be the one to build the temple. David reminded Solomon of what God called him to do, and he reminded him to keep the law of the Lord, emphasizing the promise of God's presence.

The remaining chapters detail more of the preparations for the temple. David worked hard to prepare, though he would not be the one to execute the plan. David helped to organize the priests—known as the Levites—and musicians who would serve in the temple. This was an important moment in the history of Israel, and no detail was too small.

Despite his sin, David left a legacy of loving the Lord with his whole heart. It is interesting for us to note the timing of the promise made to David in the Davidic Covenant. The promise was made that his son would build the temple before his sin. Before David ever sinned with Bathsheba or took a census, the Lord had spoken that it would be Solomon, the son of Bathsheba and David, who would build this great temple for the Lord. God was not surprised by David's sin, and He redeemed every part of David's story for His glory. In the same way, Romans 5:8 tells us that it was while we were still sinners that Christ died for us. The promised Son of David redeemed His people, not because they were good but because of His great love.

And through it all, God promised that He would dwell with His people. This is the reminder that David gave to Solomon as he prepared to build the temple, and it is echoed on every page of Scripture. God longs to dwell with His

"God longs to dwell with His people."

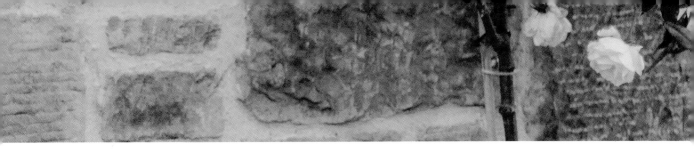

people. We see this in the garden temple of Eden and in the Old Testament tabernacle and temple. We also see it in Jesus who came to tabernacle, or dwell, among His people (John 1:14). Finally, we see it in the people of God today who are living temples of our Holy God.

QUESTIONS

Spend some time reading Psalm 30. How does this psalm enlighten your understanding of David's experience during this time of great forgiveness?

Read 1 Chronicles 22:9, and then go back and read 1 Kings 5:4. How does it grow your affection for the Lord to see Him continually fulfill His promises?

Chapters 23-25 deal with the organization of Levites, priests, and musicians. What does this show you about the attention and calling that the Lord gives to His church in worship?

1 Chronicles 22-25

The end of 1 Chronicles gives us a clear and beautiful picture of the legacy that David left.

David prepared everything for building the great temple—from organizing gatekeepers to guard and protect, to assigning treasurers to count gifts and spoils of battle. Though David would not be the one to build the temple, he worked hard to do his part in service to the Lord. The listing of so many names of those involved in the temple's work shows the importance of every person and their giftings in service to the Lord. All of God's people were valued and important in the proper worship of the Lord.

With the preparations for building coming to a close, David would give a final charge to Israel and Solomon. He encouraged the people to trust God's plan and follow Solomon, who would be their new king. And he reminded the people of God's covenant promises to establish His kingdom forever. He urged them to remember the promises of the Lord and to keep all of His commandments.

David also gave another charge to Solomon and reminded him to love and trust in the Lord alone. David reminded Solomon of the grave consequences of disobedience to God's law. David handed Solomon the plans for the great temple and urged him to be strong and courageous in service to the Lord. God chose Solomon for a great task, but He would also fill and equip him to do it. Finally, David gave Solomon a promise of the Lord's presence.

Offerings were then brought into the temple as David reminded the people that their work was not for man but the Lord. David modeled generosity as he gave of his wealth for building the temple and then encouraged the people to give for the temple's building. And the people worshiped. David led them in prayer and praise for the work that was ahead. 1 Chronicles ends with the anointing of Solomon as king over Israel and the death of David.

The Lord would equip Solomon and the people to do the work He had called them to do. He does the same for us. God would fulfill every promise that He made—from the building of the temple to the building of His kingdom. Most importantly, God would fulfill His promise to send Jesus, the Son of David, to rule and reign over His people. David was a great king who would leave a huge impact on the nation of Israel. His life served the great purpose of pointing to one better than himself. His life points to Jesus, the promised Son, who would be the fulfillment of every promise.

Reread 1 Chronicles 28:9. How does this encourage you toward obedience to God?

Meditate on David's prayer in chapter 29. What themes do you notice within the prayer?

Now that we have finished 1 Chronicles, reflect on the ways your knowledge of the Lord has grown. In what ways have your relationship and walk with the Lord been strengthened through reading this book?

May the Lord
his God
be with him.

2 Chronicles

GENERE: *Historical Narrative*

AUTHOR / DATE WRITTEN

Unknown, possibly Ezra • *c. 450-425 BC*

MAJOR THEMES — *Rebellion of Kings, Remembering History, Return from Exile into Fidelity to God*

KEY WORDS — *Exile, Return, Repentance*

KEY VERSE

2 CHRONICLES 36:23

This is what King Cyrus of Persia says: The Lord, the God of the heavens, has given me all the kingdoms of the earth and has appointed me to build him a temple at Jerusalem in Judah. Any of his people among you may go up, and may the Lord his God be with him.

2 Chronicles 1-3

2 Chronicles begins with the reign of Solomon, David's son.

From the start of the book, it is clear the Lord is with Solomon, just as the Lord was with his father. When the Lord came to Solomon to see what Solomon desired from the Lord, Solomon's answer was a plea for wisdom to rule the people who God had placed in his care. The Lord granted Solomon's humble request. Sadly, chapter 1 also records some tragic truths about Solomon. Though he was doing well in so many areas of his life, there were also areas of disobedience. Solomon was multiplying wealth and imported Egyptian horses, something the law directly prohibited kings from doing.

2 Chronicles also details the final preparations for building the temple, which included obtaining cedar from Tyre. In chapter 2, the king of Tyre makes the statement that God gave Solomon to the people as a king because He loved them. What a testament to Solomon's kingship! Solomon was a gift of love to the people of God. On the mountain that his father David had bought, Solomon begins to build the temple to replace the tabernacle that had been God's temporary dwelling place.

It was finally time to build the promised temple, and the building process is recorded in chapter 3. The holy place was built as a place for God's dwelling to rest with His people. Every detail was set forth just as the Lord had instructed. With the gifts of the people, it was a place of beauty and worship.

Just as God gave His people Solomon because of His love for them, He has given us Jesus because of His love for us. Solomon points us to the better King. Luke 11:31 tells us that there was one greater than Solomon, and this was Jesus. As mentioned before, Solomon built the temple on Mount Moriah that David had purchased for its building. It was on the same mountain that Abraham had been willing to sacrifice Isaac (Genesis 22), and it was on another section of that same mountain that Jesus would become the ultimate sacrifice once and for all for the sins of His own. God was working through every step of the story to bring about His plan for our redemption.

2 Chronicles begins by saying that the Lord was with Solomon and "highly exalted him." What does this tell you about the importance of closeness with God?

Reflect on the words of the King of Tyre in 2 Chronicles 2:11-12. What are some of the ways that God used David and Solomon to bear witness to His own glory?

Reread chapter 3. As you read about the temple constructed, keep Ephesians 2:21-22 in mind. How does your understanding of the physical temple described in chapter 3 inform your understanding of the new temple created through Christ — that is the Church?

2 Chronicles 4-6

As God had promised, Solomon would complete the building of the temple.

He would construct and furnish it just as the Lord had specified. They would bring the ark in, and the glory of the Lord would fill the temple. Can you imagine the celebration that must have taken place that day? The Lord kept His covenant and did what He said that He would do. His presence filled the temple, and God's dwelling place was with the people just as the Lord promised.

In chapter 6, the text records Solomon blessing the people and his beautiful prayer of dedication for the temple. Solomon began by recounting the covenant that God made with David. Remembering the covenant was something that God's people were reminded to do often. This takes place through feasts and special moments like the one recorded in chapter 6. The promise of the covenant would be spoken to the people as a way of remembering what God said He would do, what He had already done, and what they could trust Him to do in the future. The prayer includes mention of foreigners coming to love the Lord and even of the coming exile if the people disobeyed. Throughout this blessing and prayer, the theme of God's faithfulness to His covenant is repeated over and over again. It is a reminder that God does what He says He will do. He keeps His promises, and His steadfast love endures forever.

God was faithful to allow the temple to be built under Solomon. If He had been faithful to that aspect of the covenant, the people could rest assured that God would also be faithful to bring about the greater Son of David promised in the covenant. He would bring the One who would reign on the throne forever and whose kingdom would have no end.

2 Chronicles 6:18 contains an interesting question in Solomon's prayer when he asks if God will dwell with man on earth. Perhaps Solomon would have been shocked to find out that the answer was "Yes!" Jesus would come as God Himself, robed in flesh to dwell with the people He created. The greatest fulfillment of the Davidic covenant would not be a beautiful temple but the beautiful Savior who came to earth to live perfectly in our place and die to pay the price for our sin. Jesus is the greatest fulfillment of every covenant promise.

"Jesus is the greatest fulfillment of every covenant promise."

60

Notice the noted material in 2 Chronicles 4:21 — "purest gold." Why do you think the quality of the gold was important? What do you think this reflects?

In chapter 5, we catch a glimpse of the glory of the Lord filling the temple while the worshipers sing praises. Reread 5:13-14. In what ways does this grow your understanding of worship and the glory of God?

Meditate on 6:32-33. How does this expand your knowledge of the accessibility of God for all who desire to come to know Him?

2 Chronicles 7-9

With the final words of Solomon's prayer of dedication for the temple, the text says that fire came down from heaven to consume the burnt offering, and the glory of God filled the new temple.

The people offered sacrifices and worshiped the Lord for His faithful and steadfast love. God was faithful to His covenant, and the temple of Solomon stood as a marker of God's covenant love and faithfulness to His people and His promises.

Soon after Solomon finished the building of the temple, the Lord appeared to Solomon with a warning. The Lord warned Solomon not to become complacent now that the temple was built. He warned him not to turn to idols or allow the people to walk away from God's commands. The warning was heavy. If the people did not obey, there would be consequences. The people would be plucked out of their land and ripped away from the beautiful, completed temple. God pleaded with Solomon for Israel, and He reminded them of His faithfulness to them. He had kept His covenant, He had delivered them from Egypt, and He had been with them through every step of their journey.

The word of the Lord would prove true as glimpses of idolatry begin to appear in the text almost immediately. Solomon's list of accomplishments includes things that kings were specifically commanded by the law not to do, like multiply horses and chariots from Egypt. The text even points out how Solomon made his wife, Pharaoh's daughter, her own house so that she would not be near the ark and its holiness. With all of Solomon's wisdom in leadership—that even the Queen of Sheba notices—Solomon had many blind spots in the areas of women and wealth. The people were slipping away from the Lord, and it was their king who was leading them.

How interesting to note that the Queen of Sheba brought gold and spices as gifts for the king of Israel. Many scholars point out that these spices would have been things like frankincense and myrrh. Solomon was a king who accomplished many good things, but he was also a man of many flaws. However, his life points us to a greater king. This King would also be brought gifts of gold, frankincense, and myrrh. And this King would have no flaws. He would lay down His life for His people and would go the cross for their sake. Every chapter of the story points us to Jesus, who is the King our hearts long for.

"Every chapter of the story points us to Jesus, who is the King our hearts long for."

Reread 2 Chronicles 7:14. What does this tell you about prayer? In what ways does this verse encourage you to know that God hears us?

In 2 Chronicles 8:16, we see the official statement that Solomon has completed the temple. How does this verse encourage you? Do you truly believe that the Lord will keep His promises to you in the same way He kept them to David and Solomon?

In 2 Chronicles 9:23, we see how the world valued the wisdom that the Lord gave Solomon. Read 2 Peter 1:3. How does this verse grow your understanding that we too have access to the Lord's wisdom and knowledge through studying the Bible?

2 Chronicles 10-12

Every king that Israel had would be measured against David.

Sadly, his grandson, Rehoboam, who was the son of Solomon, would be an example of what happens when pride consumes our lives. Rehoboam may have felt like he was living in the shadow of his father and grandfather, and perhaps he just wanted to make a name for himself. Either way, his reign would be characterized by pride, idolatry, and division. Examples of this pride are seen throughout Rehoboam's life. The text recounts how he rejected the counsel of older and wiser men in favor of reigning with an iron fist. He was a leader who did not listen or have compassion for the people he was leading. He was concerned only with how they could serve him.

The beginning of chapter 12 explicitly states that when he established himself and his own kingdom, he abandoned the law of the Lord. He took wives and bore sons whom he spread throughout all the districts of the land to rule. And when his heart turned away from the Lord, the people of Israel followed his lead. Then, the text tells us that their unfaithfulness resulted in the attack of Egypt. Egypt plundered them, but Jerusalem was spared. While there is a tiny glimmer of humility in Rehoboam's life in 2 Chronicles 12:12, where we see that the Lord turned His wrath from him, Rehoboam's life was marked by rebellion and wickedness. Scripture records him as a king who did evil in the sight of the Lord and points out that he did not set his heart to seek the Lord.

Yet even during the rule of this wicked king, God preserved Israel's faithful remnant. When others were following idolatrous priests who were worshiping at the high places and sacrificing to goat idols, there was a remnant of people who were faithful to the Lord and came to Jerusalem to sacrifice to Him. In the midst of wickedness and unfaithfulness, the remnant people of God did not waver.

Rehoboam was a king who was harsh and led in pride. But Jesus is an altogether different kind of king. He is gentle and lowly. He is humble and compassionate. He is strong and faithful. The very worst kings of Israel make our hearts long for a better king. And Jesus is the greatest King our hearts could know. Following the leader can have disastrous consequences when under the rule of a bad king, but when Jesus is the King, following Him wholeheartedly is always the right choice.

In chapter 10, we read about Rehoboam forsaking the wise counsel.
How does this chapter illustrate the importance of listening to godly advice?

Read 2 Chronicles 12:12 and 2 Chronicles 12:14 back-to-back, and compare
and contrast the two. What can we learn from this contrast?

In 2 Chronicles 12:6-7, we see the importance of humility before the Lord.
Spend some time in self-reflection. Do you find it easy or difficult to humble
yourself before the Lord?

2 Chronicles 13-15

The nation would face good years and bad years, and there would be godly kings and ungodly kings.

Through it all, God's love and commitment to His people would never waver. He would keep the covenant with His people, and if they sought Him, they would find Him. These chapters remind us again of this truth.

Abijah was not a godly leader, but when he called on the Lord for help in battle, the Lord showed up for the nation. God's faithfulness to the covenant is seen in many unexpected ways throughout the story of Scripture. This faithfulness is dependent on the Lord and His faithfulness, not on the lack of humanity's faithfulness.

Abijah's son, Asa, would then rule Judah as a godly leader for the large part of his reign. Asa would turn the hearts of the people back to the Lord and have them remember and renew their covenant with the Lord. Asa knew that there was no one like the Lord and that each battle should be fought for the glory of His name. He took away foreign altars and broke down high places and shrines. 2 Chronicles 14:5 points out that under his reign, the kingdom had peace and rest. Asa was a king who cried out to the Lord in prayer and fervently prayed for the Lord's help. And the Lord heard his pleas. Asa was encouraged by the word of the Lord that came through Azariah that the Lord was with him. Several times in these chapters, we are reminded of the truth that when we seek the Lord, He will be found (2 Chronicles 15:2-4, 15). God was consistently calling the people to turn to Him. He desired for them to repent and follow His commands. There would be consequences for sin, but there would be great blessing in following the Lord. Though many of the chapters of the Old Testament show the people turning away from the Lord, there are chapters like these that show when the people repented and turned to the Lord, He was always there.

This truth is just as powerful for us as it was for the people that day. No matter what we have done, when we turn to the Lord, we will find Him. Through Jesus and the power of the gospel, we can turn to the Lord. His grace and mercy provided a sacrifice for our sin and a plan of redemption and restoration. As believers today, God calls us to turn to Him in repentance.

Reread 2 Chronicles 13:18. What does this tell you about the nature of God? How does this expand your understanding of how much we need Him?

In what ways does 2 Chronicles 14:11 instruct us on how to pray?

Meditate on 2 Chronicles 15:2-4. How does this encourage you to pursue God more and resist sin?

2 Chronicles 16-18

Though Asa lived a life of following the Lord, in the end, he failed to trust the Lord and placed his faith in power and politics.

The final years of Asa's life were characterized by pride. He refused to turn to the Lord, even through military defeat and a diseased foot. Though he was a king who accomplished so many good things, the end of his story is a tragic reminder of the infiltrating impact of pride.

Asa's son, Jehoshaphat, would follow him and be a godly leader. Jehoshaphat walked in the ways of David. He sought the Lord and, under his rule, tore down the high places, and the law of the Lord was taught throughout his reign. While Judah had some good kings, Israel had all bad kings. Chapter 18 recounts how Jehoshaphat had political alliances with the evil King Ahab from the northern kingdom of Israel. The text introduces the prophet Micaiah, also referenced in 1 Kings 22, and emphasizes that King Ahab was not a fan of his because his prophecies were always bad news for the evil king. Micaiah talks about how the people of Israel were scattered like sheep without a shepherd. Ahab was not pleased by Micaiah's words. But the prophecy of Micaiah did indeed come true. However, the Lord protected the good King Jehoshaphat in battle, and just as the prophet had predicted, the evil King Ahab was killed in battle.

The people of Israel were like sheep without a shepherd. Their leaders had not led in righteousness and truth. But, a true and better shepherd for the people of God was coming. The Good Shepherd is Jesus, and He would be the better King for the people of God.

So many of these kings, even the best ones, were tempted by power and pride. It is easy for us to be tempted to rely on our own strength to seek power and prestige, and yet we know that it is far better to trust the Lord than our own strength (Psalm 20:7). As believers, we are not immune to the temptation of placing our faith in ourselves and seeking to control things. We must constantly remind ourselves to place our trust in the Lord alone. He is worthy of our trust, and He will never leave His people. He is the Shepherd and the King we so desperately need.

"We must constantly remind ourselves to place our trust in the Lord alone."

Spend some time in self-examination in light of 2 Chronicles 16:9. What practical steps can you take in your life to pursue a blameless heart toward the Lord?

Reread 2 Chronicles 17:6. Why might taking down the "high places and Asherim" be a courageous act? What can we learn about courage and obedience to the Lord from this verse?

In 2 Chronicles 18:7, we see the attitude of King Ahab toward the prophets who speak from God. Do you find yourself hating conviction from the Lord as Ahab did? Spend some time in prayer, asking that God would give you a love for His instruction and discipline in your life.

2 Chronicles 19-21

Chapter 19 records Juhu telling King Jehoshaphat that his alliance with Ahab was evil.

Jehoshaphat seems to repent and turn his course and the entire nation back to the Lord. In Chapter 20, when Jehoshaphat is afraid of the enemies around him, he runs to the Lord. He remembered and recounted God's covenant faithfulness to His people and asked the Lord to intercede on their behalf. The people cried out to the Lord, saying that they did not know what to do but that their eyes were on Him. The Lord comforted the people with the truth that there was no need to fear because the Lord was with them, and the battle was the Lord's. The people would not need to fight this battle, for the Lord would fight for them. God commanded them to stand still and see the Lord's deliverance. They went out to battle, but just as the Lord had said, they did not need to fight the battle because the Lord was with them, and Israel's enemies began to fight each other. God had been faithful to His word.

Sadly, at the end of Jehoshaphat's reign, he again allied with an evil king. When Jehoshaphat died, his son, Jehoram, began to reign. Jehoram was an evil king. The text points out that he was evil like the kings of Israel. But 2 Chronicles 21:7 states that despite the evil king reigning over the house of Judah, the Lord was not willing to destroy the house of David because of the covenant that He had made with David. God would not break His promises. Salvation would come through this broken family tree. Though the Lord would be faithful to His covenant, evil would still be punished, Jehoram would face the judgment of the Lord, and the final verses of chapter 21 tell us that no one regretted this king's death.

Despite the wickedness of many of Judah's kings, the Lord would not break His covenant promises. He would send deliverance through a son of David. Jesus would come just as God promised. Jesus will redeem His people and be the prophet, priest, and king for whom all of the Old Testament causes us to desire.

Like the people of Judah praying to the Lord for direction, we can ask the Lord to lead us, even when we do not know what to do. We can rest in the truth of His covenant faithfulness to us, knowing that He will never break His covenant. We can walk in faithfulness, not because of the power of our strength but because of the strength of Jesus Christ in us.

"We can rest in the truth of His covenant faithfulness to us."

What does the "terror of the Lord" mean, as stated in 2 Chronicles 19:7? How does fearing the Lord benefit our walk with Him? Read Proverbs 9:10 for additional understanding.

Meditate on 2 Chronicles 20:15-17. How does it comfort you to know that the Lord will accomplish victory on our behalf? How does this grow your understanding of God's sovereignty?

In chapter 21, we learn about the wickedness of Jehoram. In verse 20, we read that he was not honored by Judah in his death and that he "died to no one's regret." What does this tell you about the impact that sin and wickedness have on those surrounding you.

2 Chronicles 22-24

The evil plans of men will never destroy the perfect plan of the Lord.

This theme is repeated throughout the pages of Scripture. Today's passage opens with Ahaziah reigning in Judah. He is the youngest son of Jehoram, and he is evil like his father before him. We are also introduced to his mother, Athaliah, who Scripture describes as his counselor in wickedness (2 Chronicles 22:3). Ahaziah was not on the scene long when Scripture records that God ordained his downfall. God executed His sovereign judgment over Ahaziah by bringing down this evil king.

The evil queen mother, Athaliah, was determined to destroy the line of David and ultimately the line of the Messiah. But God had other plans. God so often uses the unexpected and unlikely ones to bring about His plan and remind us that He is in control. God uses a woman named Jehoshabeath to rescue the baby Joash, the last remaining heir forgotten by the evil queen. Jehoshabeath was the daughter of Jehoram and the wife of the priest, Jehoida. She was an unlikely and unexpected rescuer of Judah.

In patience and faith, Jehoida and Jehoshabeath waited six years with the young Joash, hiding him in the temple before the evil Athaliah was killed and the seven-year-old boy was made king. The line of David and the line of the Messiah were protected by a brave woman and her husband and a faithful and sovereign God. Joash was made king and was listed as a good king who did what was right in the eyes of the Lord. The text also describes the faithful service of the priest, Jehoida. He served the Lord faithfully and made a covenant between himself and the people that they would be faithful to the Lord. Idolatrous altars and images were broken down, and the people worshiped the Lord with singing and rejoicing. Joash also instituted repairs to be done to the Lord's temple. Sadly, after Jehoida died, Joash was influenced by the rulers of Judah, and he abandoned the house of the Lord and broke the Lord's commandments.

God is always faithful to bring about His plan. God used a young woman to protect the promised line of David and at just the right time brought the

new king to the scene. In much the same way, Jesus was the promised King for whom the world waited. He was the reason for God's promise to the line of David, and at just the right time, God brought forth the Messiah to ransom a people for God and fulfill His plan of redemption.

QUESTIONS

How does it comfort you to know that Athaliah could not thwart the plan of God to bring the Messiah out of the lineage of King David?

Jehoiada waited seven years before he took the courage to reveal Joash. What does this tell you about seasons of waiting?

We learn from the interaction between Joash and Zecheriah (2 Chronicles 24:20-22) that proclaiming truth is not always well received. Why is proclaiming the word of the Lord important regardless of how it is received?

2 Chronicles 25-27

These chapters continue to record the kings of Judah.

The first king recorded in 2 Chronicles 25 is Amaziah. He was the son of Joash, and though Scripture says that he did what was right in the eyes of the Lord, Scripture also points out that he did not do so wholeheartedly. He came to the throne and immediately killed the servants who had gone up against his father. However, Scripture records that he did not kill the children of the conspirators according to the law. The text also records him achieving military victory. While preparing for battle, he paid to have the army of Israel join him, but a man of God stepped in and warned him not to have the enemy army join in battle. Though Amaziah lost the money that he had paid, he achieved the victory that the Lord promised. Sadly, he also had many failures, and the text records that after conquering enemy armies, he began to worship the false gods of the people he had conquered. As a result of his idolatry, the Israelite army defeats him.

His son, Uzziah, was next on the throne of Judah. Uzziah began his reign at just sixteen years of age, and the text again states that he did what was right in the eyes of the Lord. He sought the Lord and the prophet Zechariah instructed him. Unfortunately, once he was strong, pride overcame him. He went into the temple to offer incense, which was something that was reserved for the priests. He was struck with leprosy as a consequence of his disobedience and lived the rest of his life with the disease. His son, Jotham, was the final king recorded in this section of Scripture, and he too was a king described as doing right in the eyes of the Lord. He ordered his life in the way of the Lord, and God rewarded him for it.

These chapters remind us of the importance of guarding our hearts and keeping our hearts pure before the Lord. These chapters chronicle three kings who, though they had good aspects, also did things to displease the Lord. We are reminded of the importance of following the Lord with our whole hearts. Amaziah, Uzziah, and Jotham are all listed as kings who did what was right in the sight of the Lord, and yet they struggled with idolatry, pride, and incomplete obedience. Jesus is our perfect example of a perfect king. He is the King we look to and the King we serve. Through Him, we learn to live and serve from humility and not pride, and it is only through Him that we too can do what is right in the eyes of the Lord.

Reread 2 Chronicles 25:14-16. How does this passage inform your understanding of the importance of listening to wise counsel?

In 2 Chronicles 26:16, we learn that Uzziah's pride led to his destruction. What does this tell you about the importance of humility?

2 Chronicles 27:6 tells us that Jotham became mighty because he "did not waver in obeying the Lord his God." What do you think that means? What are some practical steps that we can take to ensure we are ordering our ways before the Lord?

2 Chronicles 28-30

The importance of leadership is a lesson intertwined through the stories of the kings of Israel and Judah.

Evil kings turned the hearts of the people away from the Lord, but godly kings encouraged the hearts of the people and turned them to the Lord.

Ahaz was an evil king who did not do what was right in the eyes of the Lord. He promoted idolatry, shut down temple worship, and even promoted and participated in child sacrifice. His actions caused the defeat and captivity of Judah. The text states that the Lord gave Judah into the hands of Syria. Israel came to take captives from Judah, but the prophet Oded stepped in to warn Israel of their sin and the consequences of enslaving their relatives from Judah. Ahaz continued to spiral out of control, and as the nation was in distress, he became more and more faithless. The judgment for his wickedness should have turned him to the Lord, but instead, his heart was hardened. He continued sacrificing to the foreign gods of the nations that had conquered him, and he filled Judah with high places for idol worship.

The son of Ahaz was an altogether different kind of king and one of the best kings that Judah would ever know. Hezekiah did what was right in the eyes of the Lord and is described as a king like David. He cleansed the temple, restored the temple worship, and brought the people together to celebrate the Passover for the first time in a long time. The high places were torn down, and the evil that Ahaz instituted was systematically dismantled.

Under Hezekiah, the people were called to repentance and to return to the Lord their God. The remnant of the people of God were urged to turn their hearts to their covenant God, yield to Him, come to His sanctuary, and serve Him alone. The people were reminded that the Lord is gracious and merciful and would not turn from them if they returned to Him. The result was great joy in Jerusalem and the Lord hearing the prayers of His people.

The covenant promises of God are made possible for us only through Jesus Christ. It is in Him that we can fully comprehend the grace and mercy of God. And it is through Him that we find joy everlasting. The goodness of Jesus should turn our hearts to worship just as it did in Judah so many years ago. Grace and mercy are found in Him alone.

In 2 Chronicles 28:22, we see that "at the time of his distress, King Ahaz himself became more unfaithful to the Lord." Spend some time in self-examination. Do you allow distress to drive you away from the Lord, or do you cling to Him in hardship?

Think about the fact that Hezekiah cleansed the temple. What do you think the importance of this is?

Meditate on 2 Chronicles 30:9. What do you learn about God from this verse? What do you learn about His desires for His children?

2 Chronicles 31-33

Hezekiah's reign is a highlight in Judah's story.

His heart followed after the Lord, and the people followed him in righteousness. Chapter 31 begins with Hezekiah breaking down high places and altars and organizing the priests who would serve the Lord and the people of God. This chapter also details how the people gave generously and abundantly to the work of the Lord.

In chapter 32, we are introduced to Sennacherib, the king of Assyria, who invaded Judah. Hezekiah encouraged the people not to fear and to trust in the Lord their God who would be with them every step of the way. But Sennacherib spoke against the Lord and tried to convince the people to turn away from God and place their faith in him. He sought to instill fear in the people of Judah by telling them that God would not protect them and neither would Hezekiah. But the Lord delivered the people of Judah just as He had promised and just as Hezekiah said He would. Sadly, chapter 32 ends with mentions of Hezekiah's pride in his later years. Failure to follow the Lord in the final years of life has become a tragic recurring theme throughout the kings of Judah.

After Hezekiah's death, his son, Manasseh, took the throne. Manasseh began to reign at just twelve years old, and he was an evil king. He rebuilt the high places that his father had torn down, placed idols in the temple, and even offered his own sons as burnt offerings. And the people followed him in wickedness. The text states that under him, the people of Judah became more evil than the enemy nations the Lord had destroyed. But there is a glimmer of hope in Manasseh's story. Despite all of his evil and wickedness, he humbled himself and came to the Lord in repentance. God heard his plea for mercy and received him with open arms. But even though Manasseh repented, the people continued to live wickedly. And Amon would be another evil king who continued to lead the people in wickedness.

King after king ruled in Judah. Some were good kings. Some were evil kings. But all of them were flawed kings. The kings of Judah make us long for the King of Judah. Jesus is the only perfect King. He is the only one who can perfectly meet God's holy law and the only one who can lead us in truth and righteousness.

Reread 2 Chronicles 31:20-21. How does reading about Hezekiah's life encourage you to obey and serve the Lord?

In 2 Chronicles 32:8, we read about the confidence we have when we hope in the Lord rather than our flesh. Do you find it difficult to put your confidence in the Lord? Spend some time in prayer, asking that God would grow your confidence in Him.

Compare and contrast Manasseh from the first half of chapter 33 to the second half. In what ways does this radical change encourage you?

2 Chronicles 34-36

As the book of 2 Chronicles ends, we are reminded again that the nation would rise and fall on leadership.

This last section records the triumph of the great king, Josiah, who personally experienced the Lord and the power of His Word and then turned the entire nation to the Lord. This young king was one of Judah's best kings, and the text records that he walked in the ways of the Lord just as David did. The book of the law was found in the temple. Had the people even noticed that it was missing? But King Josiah sought the Lord. The Word of the Lord moved him to repentance, and it changed the way that he led the people of Judah. Josiah sent for the prophetess Huldah, and she helped them understand the Word of the Lord.

Josiah gathered the people of Judah and read the words of the book of the covenant to them, and the king made a covenant with the Lord. Josiah would follow the Lord with his whole heart and soul, and he would lead the people to do the same. He tore down the high places and kept the Passover. He encouraged the priests to serve the Lord. Under Josiah's leadership, the nation followed the Lord and kept His commandments.

Unfortunately, the decline of Judah would come after Josiah's death as evil kings would reign again in Judah. The Lord, in His compassion, had sent prophets to warn the people of Judah of the devastation that would come if they turned from the Lord, yet they continued in their sin. Eventually, the people fell into captivity just as the prophets prophesied.

However, the book ends with a glimmer of hope and a proclamation from Cyrus of Persia that a remnant of God's people would return to the land. Even when all hope seemed lost, the Lord was there, keeping His covenant with His people, ready to restore them. He is a God of restoration and redemption. We see this clearly in Jesus Christ, who is the King for whom our hearts long. He is the one who returns us to God, who created us for His glory. It is in Him alone that we find hope, compassion, and rest. Though the story of God's people recorded in the books of Kings and Chronicles is tragic, it points us to Jesus, who is our only hope.

"It is in Him alone that we find hope, compassion, and rest."

What can we learn from Josiah being changed by the scroll of God's Word found in the temple? Do you believe in the transformative power of your Bible?

What does 2 Chronicles 36:15-16 tell you about the importance of listening to God? What does it tell you about the compassion of God?

Now that we have completed reading 2 Chronicles, spend some time in reflection over what you have learned. What has been the most impactful to you through reading this book?

a great shout
of praise to
the Lord

Ezra

GENRE: *Historical Narrative*

AUTHOR / DATE WRITTEN
Likely Ezra • c. 460-400 BC

 MAJOR THEMES — *God's Covenant Faithfulness, Redemption of God's People into the Promised Land, Returning to Proper Worship of the Lord*

 **KEY WORDS** — *Rebuild, Faithfulness, Obedience, Worship*

KEY VERSE

EZRA 3:11

They sang with praise and thanksgiving to the Lord: "For he is good; his faithful love to Israel endures forever." Then all the people gave a great shout of praise to the Lord because the foundation of the Lord's house had been laid.

Ezra 1-3

The book of Ezra begins where the book of 2 Chronicles leaves off — with the people in captivity, the temple destroyed, and a proclamation from Cyrus, king of Persia.

Isaiah prophesied the captivity, and Jeremiah had prophesied that it would last seventy years. Every word the prophets spoke came to pass, and yet again, God had kept His promises. The book of Ezra is another historical narrative, which is why it is placed in the Canon where we find it. It continues for us the story of the people of God.

The Lord actively kept His promises despite Israel's time in captivity. He was stirring hearts to bring about His plan. From the foreign King Cyrus to the people of God, it was the Lord who stirred hearts to rebuild His house in Jerusalem. The people who had been exiled would at last return to Jerusalem. Their suffering would not last forever. The Lord would deliver just as He said.

When the people returned and settled back into their homeland, the work of rebuilding would begin. It would start with the rebuilding of the altar and the temple for the worship of the Lord. And with the completion, there would be sacrifices made to the covenant God who had been with them every step of their journey. As the foundation stones were laid, the people began to sing and give praise and thanks to the Lord as they said, "For he is good; his faithful love to Israel endures forever" (Ezra 3:11). The people of Israel had long been unfaithful to the Lord, as is chronicled in the Old Testament. Yet despite their persistent unfaithfulness, the Lord would not neglect His promises.

Even when we are unfaithful, He is faithful. The Lord used Cyrus, a foreign king, to fulfill His purposes. Because God rules over the affairs of men and because He is sovereign over all, He can use anyone or anything to fulfill His perfect plan. The return from exile and the rebuilding of the temple would not be easy, but it would be worth it. God's faithful love for His people would one day be fully displayed in another king, King Jesus. Jesus would be the altar and the temple our hearts needed. He would be the perfect sacrifice that brings us to the Lord. His faithful and merciful love pursues us through the person of Jesus.

"Even when we are unfaithful, He is faithful."

What are some ways you can see that reading 1 Kings and 2 Kings has prepared you to read the book of Ezra? Do you find it easier to read chapter 2 because of your understanding of Israel's history?

Meditate on the fact that God decided to use King Cyrus, not an Israelite, to fulfill His purposes. How does this display God's sovereignty? In what ways can we be comforted by God's sovereignty?

Spend some time in reflection over the importance of rebuilding the temple, particularly thinking about the worshipfulness of Israel after laying the foundation (Ezra 3:10-13). What type of hope do you think the Israelites were feeling? What can we learn about the intensity of their worship during this time?

Ezra 4-6

Though the Lord had been the one who had called them back to do this work, that did not mean that the journey would be without suffering and difficulty. The adversaries came, claiming that they worshiped Yahweh (the Hebrew name for God), but their evil schemes did not fool Zerubbabel and Jeshua. It seemed like there were adversaries on every side. The rebuilding efforts were opposed and halted completely for about fifteen years. The people must have been discouraged and confused as they had returned to the land to do what God had called them to do, only to face opposition that halted their work for the Lord.

But this work was the Lord's work. He was sovereign over every part of the journey, including the opposition. He was not taken off guard or surprised by the difficulties and opposition that they faced in their service to Him. The building eventually began again with the help of prophets like Haggai and Zechariah, who we will read more about later. They encouraged the people to trust the sovereign and faithful hand of the Lord. They declared that God would be faithful and good, and the work resumed with a renewed zeal to complete what God had called them to do.

A search was initiated for the decree from King Cyrus, and when it was found, it was confirmed that Cyrus had not only approved of the rebuilding but also offered to pay for this bigger and better temple. So chapter 6 ends with the temple being finished and dedicated to the Lord. During the celebration of the Passover and temple dedication, the people of Israel celebrated with believing Gentiles who followed Yahweh and joined the people of God.

The Old Testament declares the truths of the New Testament—that God's people are brought together from every tribe, tongue, and nation to worship the God of creation. Together they celebrated the Passover that pointed to Jesus the Messiah who would rescue His people from the bondage of sin. The journey was not easy, but the Lord was with them. Following the Lord is not a guarantee of an easy journey, but His faithfulness is sure. Our service to the King of kings will always be worth it.

"Following the Lord is not a guarantee of an easy journey, but His faithfulness is sure."

Reread Ezra 4:4-5. In what ways have you been discouraged from staying committed to the task that God has given you?

Meditate on John 16:33. What are some experiences you might have had in which you faced opposition while being obedient to the Lord? Did you allow that experience to drive you away from God or cling to Him?

At the close of chapter 6, we see the temple finished and the celebration of Passover. What significance do you think there is to the Passover taking place at this time?

Ezra 7-10

In chapter 7, we are introduced to Ezra for whom this book of the Bible is named.

The text tells his family history and that he was a scribe who knew well the law of Moses. Yet, there is one phrase—one that is perhaps the best description of Ezra—that repeatedly occurs through the remainder of the book. The text states that the hand of the Lord his God was upon him. Though we do not have many details about Ezra's story and background, these words help us understand the kind of man he was. The king of Persia, Artaxerxes, sent Ezra and all who wished to go with him to Jerusalem. The king gave them protection and financial aid in accomplishing this great task. The Lord's hand was upon Ezra as he led the people to Jerusalem, a place which he had likely never been. As the people began to journey, Ezra sent back for the Levites and fasted and prayed for protection on the journey.

The people were beginning to turn their hearts to the Lord, but for so long, their hearts had followed after their desires. God commanded His people not to marry foreigners. The sole reason for this declaration was because those of other lands did not worship Yahweh but worshiped foreign idols. With the realization of the sin of Israel, Ezra prayed. He confessed and wept as he asked God for mercy. The confession shown in the passage is both corporate and personal. The people confessed their personal sins, but they also confessed the sins of their nation and even the sins of their ancestors who had gone before them and lived wickedly. Yet through all of their sin and brokenness, the Lord their God declares in chapter 9 that He had not forsaken them. He had extended His steadfast, covenant love to them and been with them every step of the way. The end of the book finds the people repenting and making some hard decisions about how to move forward. Many Bible scholars disagree about whether the decisions that were made were based on God's direction or the people's zeal. Yet as the book closes, we are reminded again of the steadfast love and mercy of God.

Ezra pointed the people to the law of God, and he wept and interceded to the Lord on their behalf. Yet, Ezra is just a picture of Jesus who would weep over the sin and unbelief of Israel and even now intercedes for His own (Luke 19:41). The book of Ezra points us to Jesus and urges us to be faithful to the One who is always faithful to us.

"The book of Ezra points us to Jesus and urges us to be faithful to the One who is always faithful to us."

88

Throughout these chapters, we are reminded that the hand of the Lord was with Ezra. How do you find comfort in God's presence with His people?

How do these chapters grow your understanding of the necessity of being "equally yoked" as said in 2 Corinthians 6:14?

Now that we have finished the book of Ezra, spend some time reflecting on what you have learned. What are some of the things that have most impacted your relationship with God?

This task had been accomplished by our God.

Nehemiah

GENRE: *Historical Narrative*

AUTHOR / DATE WRITTEN
Unknown, likely Ezra • *c. 445-420 BC*

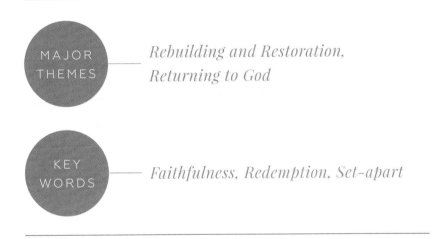

MAJOR THEMES — *Rebuilding and Restoration, Returning to God*

KEY WORDS — *Faithfulness, Redemption, Set-apart*

KEY VERSES

NEHEMIAH 6:15-16

The wall was completed in fifty-two days, on the twenty-fifth day of the month Elul. When all our enemies heard this, all the surrounding nations were intimidated and lost their confidence, for they realized that this task had been accomplished by our God.

Nehemiah 1-3

The book of Nehemiah falls near the middle of the
English Bible, and yet, chronologically, it is one of the
final pieces of the Old Testament story.

"Jesus...the true Restorer of His people."

Its main character is a man named Nehemiah. Many scholars believe that
this book was written by Ezra. That said, the events in Nehemiah take place
about fifteen years after the events recorded in the book of Ezra. While the
book of Ezra details the rebuilding of the temple, the book of Nehemiah
details the rebuilding of the wall of Jerusalem.

The account begins in Susa with a report coming back to Nehemiah, a Jew
working in the palace as the cupbearer to the king. This position has been
likened to the modern "chief of staff." When Nehemiah heard the news, he
was moved with compassion and to prayer. He wept and prayed because of
the need that he saw. This was not prayer for a moment, but a four-month
prayer prayed before he speaks to Artaxerxes, the king. After his long season
of prayer, he makes a bold request for assistance to go to Jerusalem to rebuild
the wall. So after months of prayer, he approaches the king, even though he is
overwhelmed with fear, and after one last prayer, he makes his request to the
king. In faith, he went to the Lord in prayer; in faith, he went to the king; and
in faith, he journeyed back to Jerusalem and rallied the people to join him in
rebuilding the city wall for God's glory.

Though the Lord tasked Nehemiah with this great work, he was not immune
to opposition. Opposition would come, and the task before him would at
times feel too great. Nehemiah would need to rebuild the wall meant to protect Jerusalem, and he would need to encourage a very discouraged group
of people to join him in the work. Yet by chapter 3, in what may seem like a
long list of names, we see the people of God working together to accomplish
the mission of God.

Nehemiah is a small book of the Bible, and yet in it, we are reminded to look
at the needs around us and, in compassion, respond to those needs. We are
reminded to come to the Lord in prayer and to humbly lead others to love
and serve the Lord as well. Most of all, we are pointed to Jesus, who has compassion on us, prays for us, leads us, and is the true Restorer of His people.

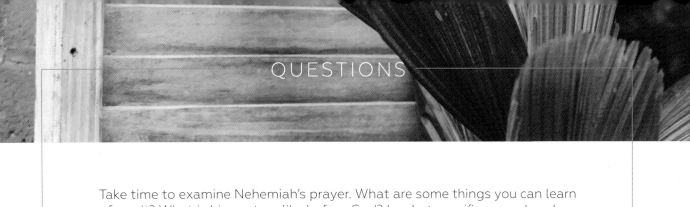

Take time to examine Nehemiah's prayer. What are some things you can learn from it? What is his posture like before God? In what specific ways does he praise God? In what ways does he offer repentance?

Reread Nehemiah 2:18. In these first three chapters, what are some ways that we have already seen God's hand upon Nehemiah?

In chapter 3, we see many people who are charged with different jobs, but all have the same common cause. In what ways does this compare to the Church?

Nehemiah 4-6

Nehemiah and the people got to work rebuilding the wall. But it would not be a completely smooth process.

It did not take long for opposition to arrive through Sanballat and Tobiah. They came with insults and accusations. Nehemiah's response should not be a surprise after what we have read about him so far. His response was to go to the Lord in prayer. He prayed, and then the text says that they kept on building. They did not let the schemes of their enemy distract them from the work that God called them to do.

Through the very real fear that the people of God experienced, they went to the Lord and prayed for Him to be with them. They remembered the Lord, and by faith in the God who had never left them, they overcame the obstacles set before them. But the opposition did not only come from the outside. There was also opposition from sin within the people. It came to light that many were oppressing the poor. Nehemiah was immediately angry upon learning this news. Yet, instead of reacting in anger, he reacted with confession. Personal and corporate confession came from the lips of Nehemiah in prayer. The end of chapter 5 describes the wealth and generosity of Nehemiah and explains how he used his wealth to bless those around him and continue God's work. With the building of the wall complete, the book shifts to the building of God's people.

When we are serving the Lord, opposition will come. Nehemiah and the rest of those who set out to rebuild the wall were not exempt from this. When opposition comes, it is easy to find ourselves fearful and discouraged. The attacks of the enemy can leave us feeling crippled with fear and discourage us from doing what God has called us to do. In his wisdom, Nehemiah encouraged the people to press on and continue the work they had been sent to do by the Lord. Nehemiah turned to the Lord in prayer and was confident that the Lord would fight for them. They did not have to fear or be discouraged because the Lord was on their side. Nehemiah points us to Jesus who has fought the battle for us and won the victory in our place. We go on with the promise that He is with us every step of the journey.

Reread Nehemiah 4:14. How does this offer you strength when you face opposition?

In Nehemiah 6:9, we see Nehemiah say, "But now, my God, strengthen my hands." Spend some time in prayer as you reflect on this verse, asking God to strengthen your hands to serve Him for His purposes.

At the end of today's reading, we see that the wall has been finished and stands as a testimony that God helped His people to accomplish it (Nehemiah 6:16). Though we may struggle, how does it comfort you to know that God will always accomplish His plans?

Nehemiah 7-9

With the wall complete, God had been faithful to do what He promised.

But the Lord was not finished building the people of God into what He called them to be. God called Nehemiah to assemble the people, and chapter 7 provides a numbering of the people. As the book shifts from the building of the wall to the building of the people, the text points out the foundation of the Word of God. A renewed passion for God's Word is a prerequisite to revival.

In chapter 8, the people listen to Scripture reading from morning until midday, and they weep in response to the Word as they realize and understand their sin and deep need for redemption. Prayer and the reading and teaching of God's Word were foundational to the transformation of the people of God. Some of the most famous words of the book of Nehemiah point out that the joy of the Lord is their strength. The people spent much time and energy building a wall around Jerusalem, but the Lord wanted them to know that He alone was their strength, refuge, fortress, and stronghold.

As the people opened the Word of God, they were reminded of what God had commanded them to do. In their reading, they saw the commandment for the Feast of Booths, and they celebrated this feast together. Chapter 9 is perhaps one of the most beautiful chapters in Scripture as it records a day-long worship service. This time of worship began with confession as the people understood and confessed their own sin and the sin of their nation. Together, they read the Word of God for hours. Instead of finding boredom in a lengthy service, they clung to every word of Scripture. And then they prayed. In fact, the majority of chapter 9 is a prayer—one that tells the story of the Old Testament, the faithfulness of God, and the wandering of His people. God had been faithful to them through every wilderness thus far. Though they rebelled against Him, in steadfast love, He came near to them over and over again, for He does not abandon His promises.

The covenant promises of Nehemiah 9 are fulfilled in Jesus. He is the Redeemer who was promised to Abraham long ago. He is the one whom the prophets of old proclaimed and the one to whom every verse of Scripture points in His keeping of all of His covenants. He is the God of steadfast love. In our wandering and the wilderness of life, He is forever faithful.

"He is the God of steadfast love."

In chapter 7, we reach another genealogy. Consider the significance of this list of names — does it encourage you to read about the homecoming of each of these exiles?

Reread Nehemiah 8:9-12. How does this passage grow your understanding of God's holiness?

Throughout chapter 9, we see various reminders of God's faithfulness to His covenant (Nehemiah 9:7-8, 9:15, 9:18-19, 9:22-23, 9:30-32). How do these verses illuminate the intensity of the final verse of chapter 9?

Nehemiah 10-13

After the worship and revival of chapter 9, chapter 10 records the signing of the covenant.

The people who had wept over their sin and worshiped the Lord for His faithfulness in the midst of their unfaithfulness now surrendered to Him. They surrendered their lives, and they surrendered to His commands. This was a call to action as the people stepped up to declare their loyalty to Yahweh. Salvation should lead to surrender. The gospel should lead to action. Faith should lead to works.

In chapters 11-12, the city of Jerusalem is repopulated. People of all kinds came to fill the city now that the wall was complete. Many of these people sacrificed greatly to come to Jerusalem. They left behind their land to live in the city and build the kingdom of God. While the lists of names are seemingly long and tedious to read, for the people in Nehemiah's day this was important as they were essentially getting credit for their faithfulness. The names of the faithful were written down, and God's people rejoiced to see their names listed as those who were faithful to the Lord. The wall was dedicated, and it was a time of joy and rejoicing for all that the Lord had done.

Though chapter 12 ends triumphantly in Jerusalem, chapter 13 flashes forward over a decade, and the result is discouraging. Sadly, the book ends with the revelation that the people had once again wandered from the Lord and were unfaithful to the covenant. This may not be entirely surprising after studying chapter 9 and knowing the history of God's people. They wandered away just as they had always done, though the Lord had been steadfast and faithful to them.

The people tried to obey, and they failed. But the book of Nehemiah points us to Jesus. He is the one who fulfills the covenant. He is the one who brings a new covenant. He is the one who said, "it is finished," as He paid the price for the wandering hearts of His own. He is the faithful one. The book of Nehemiah calls us to faithfulness and surrender. It reminds us of the great things that can be accomplished for the Lord, but ultimately, it reminds us that it is only through the power of Jesus that our faithfulness to Him is possible.

Why do you think the dedication of the wall was such a time of joy for the people?

Reflect on Nehemiah 13:30-31. How does this verse impact you, knowing all that Israel endured from 1 Chronicles until this point?

Now that we have finished reading Nehemiah, spend some time in reflection over what God has taught you about Himself. What are some ways that your relationship with God has grown from reading this book?

For such
a time
as this.

Esther

GENRE: *Historical Narrataive*

AUTHOR / DATE WRITTEN

Unknown, likely Mordecai • *c. 460-400 BC*

MAJOR THEMES

God's Sovereignty and Providential Plans

KEY WORDS

Divine Providence, Deliverance

KEY VERSE

ESTHER 4:14

If you keep silent at this time, relief and deliverance will come to the Jewish people from another place, but you and your father's family will be destroyed. Who knows, perhaps you have come to your royal position for such a time as this.

Esther 1-3

This book, set in the foreign land of Persia, never mentions the Lord. However, His providential hand is seen over and over again throughout the small historical book. The story takes place in the capital of Persia, which is the nation that conquered Babylon. The exiled people of Israel grew up in this foreign land and were torn between assimilating to the foreign culture or practicing their faith in Yahweh. The book opens during one of many feasts that take place in the book. During this feast, King Ahasuerus (Xerxes I) commands Queen Vashti to parade in front of him and his men in her royal crown. Many scholars throughout the ages, including early Jewish rabbis, interpreted this to mean that she was to come out in only her crown. Though the text does not explicitly state the details, Vashti's husband summoned her to parade in front of a group of intoxicated men as an object for their pleasure. And her refusal to appear sets the plot of the book in motion.

With his lust for power, the rash king removed her position as queen, and the search for a new queen began. From all over the land, women were sent—probably involuntary—to the palace. Once there, women were placed in the king's harem, where they would spend the rest of their lives separated from everything they knew. One by one, they were brought before the king to satisfy his desires and see if one of them may be the one he would choose to be the next queen. The weighty realities of this story go beyond the sanitized Sunday school version of the story that most are familiar with. Esther was one in a long list of women who would be concubines in the harem and perhaps later become his queen.

Esther would find favor with the king and would indeed become the queen of Persia. She was an unlikely candidate. But the book's plot does not end here. The text introduces a man named Haman. Haman created a plot to kill the Jews, and the king unknowingly signed it into law. But God was working every step of the way. In some portions of Scripture, we see God speak through thunder and mighty leaders. But in Esther, we see Him working quietly behind the scenes and using the most ordinary people to accomplish His plan.

"King Jesus is the King for whom every other king makes us long."

The book opens with a king and feast; so too does the story of Scripture end with the true King and a feast. But King Jesus is not a selfish king who uses and abuses those who serve Him. King Jesus is the King for whom every other king makes us long. He is the King who lays down His life for His own and spreads a feast for those who were once His enemies. And though His name is not mentioned in the book of Esther, each word makes us long for our true and better King.

QUESTIONS

God's name is not mentioned in this book. What does that teach you about how He sometimes works?

Beyond her beauty, Esther held the approval of the king and everyone who saw her. What does this inform us about the importance of our character?

Reread Esther 3:8-9. Was Hamen's description of the Jewish people and their laws accurate? Why is this significant?

Esther 4-6

The situation may have appeared hopeless, but the wise Mordecai trusted that the Lord would find a way to save the Jews. Mordecai knew of God's covenant with the Jews, and he knew that God would rescue His people. The Lord would be faithful to His covenant promises, and He would deliver the people of God. The Lord placed Esther where she was so that she could be used in the story that He was writing. Mordecai pleaded with her that perhaps she had become queen "for such a time as this" (Esther 4:14) Esther responded with urgency and immediately asked for the people of God to fast on her behalf.

Going before the king uninvited was dangerous, and Esther's life was at stake when she chose to enter that room. But the text tells us that Esther found favor with the king when the golden scepter was held out for her. She invited the king to a banquet instead of making her request known immediately. Meanwhile, Haman was making plans to kill Mordecai and constructing gallows to carry out his evil plans. The same night, when the king could not sleep, he was reminded of how Mordecai had saved his life (Esther 2:21-23). The king asked Haman for his opinion on the very best way to honor a man. The wicked Haman assumed that the king was going to honor him. Imagine his shock when he finished naming his elaborate plans only to be told to carry them out for Mordecai.

God's name may not be present in this book, but His providence is seen over and over again. God was working behind the scenes to save His people and bring about the promised redemption. The book of Esther is a declaration of the faithfulness of God. This faithfulness has been seen in the story of Scripture from the very first chapters of Genesis when God made a covenant and promised a redeemer. Redemption would come through Jesus who would be born generations later. But God was already working out the plan of Jesus's coming, and He was using ordinary people to do so. Mordecai's words stand out. God would save His people and keep His covenant. But perhaps He would choose to use His people to bring about His plan of redemption. Let this be the posture and prayer of our hearts in our own lives. May we live faithful lives and be used in God's story.

"May we live faithful lives and be used in God's story."

Reread Esther 4:1-4. What was the purpose of the mourning of Mordecai and the other Jewish people? What does this teach us?

In Esther 4:13-14, Mordecai has confidence that the Jewish people will be delivered yet still implores Esther to act. What does this show us of being participants in God's sovereign plan?

Reflect on Esther 6:1-14. What does this passage teach us about pride and bitterness?

Esther 7-10

Haman begged for his life, but the furious king ordered for Haman to be hanged on the same gallows he had built for Mordecai. Haman's evil plan was thwarted, and he paid the price that he had intended for Mordecai while Esther rescued the Jews with her courage. When enemies came to attack, the Jews defeated them. The fear and worry among the Jews turned to gladness and Joy (Esther 8:17). God was in the details, and on the very same day that their enemies hoped to annihilate the Jews, the Jews took victory over those who hated them (Esther 9:1). In integrity, and perhaps in memory of their past, the Jews defeated their enemies but did not take the spoils of war. God had not abandoned His people. He brought deliverance and used His people to accomplish it.

The Feast of Purim was inaugurated to celebrate the great victory and joy of that day, and Mordecai was made second to the king. God did what He said He would do—though perhaps unexpectedly, using a foreign king who did not know God to rescue His people.

God always comes through for His own. He never lets them down. He continuously works in ways that we cannot see or imagine and yet still invites us into the story of redemption that He is writing. Remember the words of Mordecai in chapter 4—God would rescue His people somehow, and we can be certain of that. What a joy to be invited, like Mordecai and Esther, into the story that God is writing. Jesus won the victory for our salvation on the cross of Calvary, and someday He will win the final fight with evil. He is our victorious King, our mighty warrior, and our strong rescuer. The hero of this story is not Mordecai or Esther but the great God whom they served.

We, too, are invited into the story of redemption that God is writing. We are called to seek and build the kingdom of God on earth. We are called to herald the good news of the gospel to those around us. We are called to be faithful in ordinary places and ordinary days. And we are called to live for eternity and the glory of our sovereign King.

"We, too, are invited into the story of redemption that God is writing."

Reread Esther 7:9. In what ways is this an example of God using for good what was intended for evil?

The people of God were saved through the efforts of Esther and Mordecai. How does this encourage you to be faithful despite great evil?

Now that you have read the book of Esther, reflect on what you have learned. Though the Lord is never mentioned in this book by name, in what ways do you see God working for the sake of His people?

Now my eyes have seen you.

Job

GENRE: *Wisdom, Narrative, Poetry*

AUTHOR / DATE WRITTEN
Unknown, possibly Moses • c. 1440 BC

MAJOR THEMES — *God's Righteousness and Governing Justice, God's Supreme Ruling and Superior Knowledge*

KEY WORDS — *Suffering, Humility, Righteousness, Justice*

KEY VERSE

JOB 42:5

I had heard reports about you, but now my eyes have seen you.

Job 1-3

The book of Job serves to remind us that God is sovereign in all things.

He is sovereign over every part of our lives, even over the suffering that we face. The book of Job asks the question, why do bad things happen to good people? It causes us to wrestle with deep questions and urges us to bring those questions to the Lord.

Job was a righteous man who served God. In fact, in Job 1:8, God refers to him as "my servant Job." He was upright and holy and a man of great wealth whose life overflowed with spiritual and physical blessings. But Satan came to God's throne seeking to accuse God's people (Revelation 12:10). God esteemed Job greatly, but Satan sought to find fault in him, convinced that if Job's possessions were taken from him, he would surely curse God. And though God allowed Satan to take from Job, He remained sovereign over it, setting boundaries on Satan that he could not cross.

Thus, everything was taken from Job, and yet his response was to worship the Lord. He recognized that everything that he had was from God and that God was always worthy of praise. Job faced great suffering, but he also had a great God. Job recognized that God is the giver and that He has the right to take as well. Next, Satan attacked Job's health, yet Job stood firm. Sadly, Job's wife and friends gave poor counsel. His wife urged him to curse God and die, and his friends gave false wisdom. Chapter 3 contains Job's lament for all that had taken place, and he goes so far as to lament being born.

The book of Job has much to teach us about suffering and the sovereignty of God. It reminds us of God's control over even the most difficult parts of our lives. It reminds us that we are to worship Him for who He is and not just what He has given us. The book of Job points us to Jesus, who bore suffering, shame, and even death in our place so that we could be called the sons and daughters of God. No matter what suffering we face, we can trust His unfailing love for us.

"No matter what suffering we face, we can trust His unfailing love for us."

As we begin to study the book of Job, we meditate on Job 1:22. Do you have the same first reaction when troubles overwhelm you? Do you cling to God and His goodness no matter what comes?

In Job 2:9-10, we see that Job still holds fast to the Lord, refusing to sin with his lips. How does this illustrate the importance of the holiness of our mouths?

The first encounter that we have with Job's three friends — Eliphaz, Bildad, and Zophar — is one of comfort and solidarity. Meditate on this encounter; do you find yourself willing to grieve with those who are suffering around you?

Job 4-6

As the book of Job continues, we see Job's friends speak to him about all that has happened, and Job responds to their advice.

"In the pain and sorrow of life, we have a place to run and a God who will not abandon us."

Job's friends certainly meant well; they came to sit with him in his grief and advise him. However, their words are rash and do not show God's heart for His people. Eliphaz speaks first, and ironically, he speaks of the power that Job's words had to encourage many others. But unfortunately, the words that Eliphaz speaks to Job do not encourage him. Instead, they do just the opposite as Eliphaz claims that Job's suffering must be due to sin in his life.

There are times when suffering is due to our sin and its consequences, but there are other times when suffering is simply the result of living in a broken and fallen world infected with sin and pain. That was the case for Job. Scripture tells us that what happened to Job is not the result of his sin. In chapter 6, Job responds. He laments. He cries out to the Lord. He knew that what was happening was not a result of his sin, but that did not mean that he knew why it was happening. Yet through it all, he did not curse God or turn away from the hope found in the Lord.

As the book continues, Job's friends proceed to be poor companions and friends to him. Though they did come to him in his time of need, they did not encourage him in this painful time. But this can point us to Jesus, who is a better friend. He is the one who "stays closer than a brother" (Proverbs 18:24). Jesus is the one who sympathizes with us in our weakness and understands everything that we face (Hebrews 4:15). He has borne the weight of the world's brokenness on His shoulders, and now He lives to intercede for us. In the pain and sorrow of life, we have a place to run and a God who will not abandon us. Jesus's name, Immanuel, means "God with us," and this is the promise to which we cling. In our sorrow, He is with us. In our suffering, He will never leave us. And even in our sin, He runs to redeem. We have a God who is faithful and true. No matter what we are facing, we can run to Him and rest in the knowledge of His presence with us every step of the way.

How does Eliphaz's response to Job encourage you to know the character of God (by knowing the Bible better) to proclaim sincere and edifying truth to those who suffer?

What does Job 6:24 teach you about the importance of desiring godly instruction?

Read Hebrews 4:15. How is Jesus a better friend?

Job 7-9

In Job 7, Job continues his lament before the Lord.

We see the deep devastation that Job felt; his heart was filled with despair over the circumstances of his life. He speaks freely about what he was feeling, and yet even in this painful lament, there are glimmers of hope in the faithful God. In Job 7:17, Job asks the Lord why He so greatly cares for mankind and even describes God as having set His heart on man. Though the Lord allowed trials and suffering to enter Job's life, God's heart was fixed in love upon His servant, Job.

Job's friend, Bildad, speaks to him next. Bildad also contends that perhaps Job or his children did something to deserve these horrible tragedies. He focuses on the attribute of God's justice as his reasoning for those conclusions. But while God is indeed just, by focusing on only one attribute of God, Bildad misses out on a fuller picture of who God is as revealed to us through Scripture. Much of what Bildad says is true yet not the complete picture of a just God who is also loving, merciful, gracious, and kind. By providing a one-sided view of God, he distorts the image of God. Bildad calls for Job to repent instead of comforting his friend with the truth of who God is.

In chapter 9, Job replies to his friend. For several verses, he declares the character of God—that His wisdom and strength are beyond human comprehension. Though He is great and mighty, Job still pleads to the Lord for mercy in His time of need. He wrestled with his devastating present reality and the truth of who God is. Yet still, we can see that Job did not curse or abandon the Lord. He did not fully understand what was happening or why it was happening, but He did not turn from the Lord.

The cross is the perfect example to us of God's love and justice perfectly reconciled. Sin had to be paid, so Jesus paid it for us. The crucifixion of Jesus that seemed like something horrible—and indeed it was a horrible death—was the very thing that would secure redemption for the people of God. In His grace and mercy, God takes things that we cannot fully understand and uses them to bring about His eternal purposes in His grand story of redemption.

Think about Bildad's inclination of looking at God's character as one-sided. Do you ever find yourself struggling to keep a balanced view of God's character?

Spend some time in prayer, asking that God would grow your knowledge and understanding of His character in a way that is pleasing to Him.

Reflect on Job 9:32-35. In what ways does Christ serve as a mediator between God and man (Hebrews 9:15)?

Job 10-12

In Job 10, Job pleas to the Lord. He laments and pours out his heart to God.

He does not understand why God has allowed this pain and devastation to come into his life, and he takes his complaint to the Lord. He asks the Lord, "Why?" We are witnesses to the intense wrestling within Job's heart. He pleads his case before the Almighty from the overflow of his weary soul, and God invites us to do the same.

The next friend to speak is Zophar in chapter 11, and it seems the advice of Job's friends only worsens. Zophar came to Job in anger, and like those that had come before him, he blames everything that has happened on Job. Again he calls for Job to repent, though the text has made it clear that Job's suffering is not a result of his sin. Zophar does not comfort his friend but instead tells him that nothing bad would happen to him if he were a better person. Zophar comes with empty advice that does not help the situation but causes further pain and suffering for Job.

In chapter 12, Job responds, knowing that God had allowed this suffering to take place. Job even uses the language that God allowed it, and although Job does not know why He has allowed it, He knows that God is abundant in wisdom and strength and can do as He pleases. God is sovereign over all. This is the truth that Job rests in, even through the pain of his suffering, and it is a truth to which we, too, can cling.

Job's friends serve as reminders to us of how to deal with the broken and the suffering. We must not put ourselves in the place of God to judge and tell them what they must do or why their suffering must be their fault. We must instead "rejoice with those who rejoice" and "weep with those who weep," as Romans 12:15 exhorts us to do. Job's friends felt that Job's relationship with God must be lacking, but they reveal their lack of understanding of God's character. Our God loves and stands with the broken and suffering (Psalm 34:18), and He will never forsake His children. Jesus exemplifies this truth so perfectly with us by identifying with us in our suffering. He does not come to us with empty promises or hurtful advice but with words that heal our souls and comfort that gives rest to our weary souls.

"Our God loves and stands with the broken and suffering."

As the book continues, we see Job lament and ask why these bad things are happening. Have you ever asked God why something is happening? How is God's sovereignty a comfort in those times?

Now that we have heard the responses from each of Job's friends, think about them in light of Romans 12:15. What sort of response should Job's friends have had?

Reflect on chapter 12 — what are some things that you have learned about God from this chapter?

Job 13-15

Chapter 13 continues Job's reply to Zophar.

Job is pointed and direct with his language when he tells Zophar that it would be wise for him to stay silent. Zophar is attempting to speak for God, and Job knows it is not a wise decision. Job 13:15 shows how tightly Job held fast to God, and it is a reminder for us as well. Though God allows us to face suffering and trials, we can still place our hope in the sovereign God who never abandons His own. On each of its pages, the book of Job declares the magnitude and weight of God's sovereignty. He is in control of all things, even the hardest circumstances that we face.

Job's reply continues in chapter 14 as well. The first verse of the chapter is a reminder that all people in all times and cultures will face trouble. This is part of the human experience and a result of living in a fallen world. Yet despite this fact, the children of God can still rest in His sovereign care, knowing that He will never abandon His own. This chapter also reminds us that our days are numbered and determined. This points again to the sovereignty of God. He knows the end from the beginning, and He knows the length of our lives. The plan has been set, and nothing can thwart what God has planned. This should be a great comfort to us as we learn to relinquish our grasps for control and rest in the sovereignty of God alone.

In chapter 15, Eliphaz comes to accuse Job. His words are harsh as he accuses Job of not fearing the Lord or thinking that he is somehow better than his friends. Job's friends had an improper perspective of who God is and how He works. They were sure that this suffering must be Job's fault, but they were wrong.

The book of Job is a lesson on the sovereignty of God. It is a reminder that His ways are so much higher than our ways. And though we do not understand them, we can trust Him. The wisdom of God is better than the wisdom of men. The world does not understand the way that the kingdom of God works. 1 Corinthians 1:18-31 speaks of God's wisdom as the work of the cross. The wisdom of God is the message of the gospel and what Jesus Christ has done. A crucified Savior does not make sense to the world, but, for the children of God, it is the hope of eternal life and union with Christ.

"The book of Job is a lesson on the sovereignty of God."

Reread Job 13:1-19. Summarize Job's response to his friends here.

Spend some time in self-examination in light of Job 13:15. Do you hope in the Lord, regardless of your circumstances?

Job 14:5 speaks of our days being determined or numbered. How does this give you confidence in the Lord?

Job 16-18

Job's friends assumed that God must be punishing Job for some sin in his life or some evil that he had done.

"We must lift our gaze to the cross of Jesus Christ to be reminded of the character of our God."

Job's journey fills many chapters, and his grief and lament are evidenced in the face of his cruelest critics. In chapter 16, Job continues to respond to the accusations leveled against him. Job even says that he could say harsh words as they do, and it seems that he is saying that he will not stoop to their level. The phrases "friendly fire" or "kicking someone while they are down" might accurately describe what is happening with Job's friends. We are given a glimpse into Job's desperate and tear-filled prayers in Job 16:16-17, and we see how he continues to run to the Lord, even though he does not understand the situation he faces. Job's lament and despair continue into chapter 17, but sadly, his despair does not stop his friends from continuing their attack cloaked as helpful advice.

In chapter 18, Bildad once again speaks. Again, his words are full of accusations against Job. He is utterly convinced that Job has committed some great sin to deserve such horrible suffering. He accuses Job of sin and unrighteousness, and his words are full of hopelessness for Job's condition. The Lord had already declared that this was not due to Job's sin, but his calloused friends refused to believe it.

We must lift our gaze to the cross of Jesus Christ to be reminded of the character of our God. Lost in our sin, we deserve the punishment and wrath of God, but this is the beauty of the cross: Jesus took the wrath of God in our place and clothes the people of God with His righteousness. God does convict and discipline His children, but it is always in love. Like Job, there may be times when we experience suffering and pain by absolutely no fault of our own. And even then, we can have the utmost confidence that God is working and will not abandon us in our hour of need. He walks with us every step of the way.

Meditate on Job 16:16-17. What does this tell you about how our posture of prayer should be while we experience suffering?

Spend some time in self-examination. Do you tend to have the same skewed understanding of God's character as Job's three friends?

What does Job's response to his friends tell you about the importance of being able to discern godly versus fleshly counsel?

Job 19-21

Chapter 19 begins with Job reflecting on the immense power of words.

He describes the words of his friends as tormenting and crushing. His friends speak hastily, and though perhaps they thought they were encouraging or helpfully admonishing him, their words only bring him pain. During Job's discourse in chapter 19, he gives a great demonstration of faith in the coming Redeemer. He speaks clearly of Jesus when he states that he knows that his Redeemer lives. The Hebrew term *ga'al* is the kinsman-redeemer we find in the book of Ruth. Job was stating in faith that he knew no matter what happened in this life, Jesus would restore and make everything right. Job looked ahead, not just at the first coming of Jesus but also to His return when He will redeem and restore everything. Job was confident that even after he died, he would see God and see the redemption and restoration of the Messiah.

In chapter 20, Zophar speaks again. It does not seem that he paid much attention to Job's last response, for his message is that the wicked will suffer. Again, he blames Job for the suffering that has come into his life.

Job replies again in the following chapter by pointing out how often the wicked prosper on this earth. Job reminds us that we cannot teach God anything. We do not always understand His ways, but He is sovereign over everything, and He is sovereign over us. There is no detail of our lives that is outside of His sovereign care. He knows our pains, troubles, and temptations. He knows what we are facing, and He does not leave us alone. Job's friends were not good friends to Him, but our Redeemer is the friend who is closer than a brother. He is Emmanuel, God with us.

When we face trials as Job did, we can have the same confidence in our Redeemer. He will rescue, redeem, and restore all that is wrong in the world. We can say, "I know that my Redeemer lives!" Through shouts of joy or tears of lament, we can be confident in our sovereign God.

Even as he suffered, think about Job's faith in proclaiming his knowledge that his Redeemer lives. What can we learn from this type of faith that Job had?

After reading through chapter 21, what are some things Job says about God that grow your understanding of His character?

Spend some time in prayer, praising God for the knowledge and understanding that our Redeemer lives!

Job 22-24

"The God of Israel, the Savior, is sometimes a God that hides Himself, but never a God that absents Himself; sometimes in the dark, but never at a distance."

– Matthew Henry

The attacks of Job's friends seem to become more vicious with each discourse. The friends who Job needed to encourage only make things worse. We see this evidenced in Eliphaz's words in chapter 22. Though some of the things that Eliphaz says are true, much of what he says simply blames Job for the suffering he faces.

Surely, Job was confused and hurting. On top of the pain and suffering that he was feeling, his friends blamed him for his life's calamity. God seemed far away. He felt that he could not find the Lord, and yet he knew that God was there. Job not only knew that God was there, but he believed that God was using this fire to refine him. This was not the first or only time in Scripture that trials are likened to fire or a furnace (Isaiah 48:10, Deuteronomy 4:20, Psalm 66:10, 1 Peter 1:6-7, 4:12). Chapters 23 and 24 give us a glimpse into Job's heart as he wrestles with God. As his faith is tested, he takes his complaints to God.

God's plan did not seem clear, and this is often the case in our own lives as well. But this is not something new. Throughout Scripture, we can see that God had a definite plan to redeem His people through His Son. Yet through much of Scripture, the plan is seen in shadow form. Glimpses of Jesus are on every page of Scripture until He enters the world in the first pages of the New Testament. God was there. He was working. But it did not always seem clear. God uses the trials and suffering of this life to make us more like Him. Just like Job, we may not know where God is, but we know He is there. We may not know what He is doing, but we know that He is still working. We may not understand His plan, but we know who He is. Our faithful Redeemer will not let us down.

"God uses the trials and suffering of this life to make us more like Him."

After reading the quote from Matthew Henry, think about the comfort and encouragement we can find in knowing that God is never distant. Spend some time in prayer, praising God that He is near.

Think about the imagery of fire and furnaces as used to describe trials. What do you think the significance of this is?

Reread Job 23:11-12. Why is it important that Job knows that he is righteous before God?

Job 25-27

In chapter 25, Bildad returns with more accusations against Job.

In the shortest of Job's friend's speeches, Bildad focuses on God's power and justice. God is all-powerful, and God is justice. But Bildad did not have a clear picture of God, and as he examines these attributes of God, he claims that suffering must be the result of sin. He seems sure that Job's suffering is a result of some evil that he committed. Bildad asks how a man can be right with God, and though Bildad's accusations are off base, his question is, nevertheless, one worth answering.

Job points out in chapters 26 and 27 that it is the Lord who sustains us. We cannot take a breath without His help. Job's reply points out that the words of Job's friends are not uplifting, and they are not from God. Job also reminds them that we cannot understand God's power or justice. His ways are higher than our ways (Isaiah 55:8-9). Though suffering exists for all people, that suffering is not necessarily due to our wrongdoing. Because we live in a world that is tainted by sin, every person will certainly feel the effects of that sin and brokenness to some degree.

Jesus is our perfect example of someone suffering who is righteous. He suffered greatly, yet there was no sin in Him. He is the example to which we should look in our suffering, for even in His deepest suffering, He never sinned. And it is because of His suffering that someday all suffering will be erased. We can find comfort in who He is and hope that someday the tears and the sorrow and the pain will end. The answer to Bildad's question regarding how a man can be right with God is found only in the person and work of Jesus Christ. Redemption is found only in the name of Jesus.

We can have hope and confidence in the power and justice of God. We can rest knowing that the Lord sustains us through every moment. We can know that God is working in ways that we cannot see to bring about His good purposes for His people and establish His kingdom on this earth.

"We can have hope and confidence in the power and justice of God."

Bildad's response to Job in chapter 25 is a picture of why it is so important to know God's character well. Take a moment for self-examination. Do you speak of God in the ways that Job does or in the ways that Bildad does?

Chapters 26 and 27 both include imagery of creation to demonstrate the power of God. Why do you think this might be significant?

Meditate on Isaiah 55:8-9. How can this verse be an encouragement to you today?

Job 28-30

True wisdom always comes from God.

"We can trust Him and know that true wisdom is found in Him alone."

He sees all and knows all. Job's friends thought they were wise, but they did not understand all that God knows and sees. Job knew that wisdom is from God, but he also struggled with his thoughts and emotions in suffering.

In chapter 28, Job continues in response to his accusers. He poses some important questions: Where is wisdom found? Where is understanding found, and how can we know what is true, right, and just? Job wrestled with the truth that he knew and the pain he was feeling. This is seen throughout the entire book of Job. Here in chapter 28, Job affirms that God alone is the place where wisdom is found. God knows. God sees everything. God has declared and established all things in His divine will. Even when we do not understand, the Lord can be trusted. Job 28:28 is a call from God asking mankind to fear the Lord—for that is wisdom—and to turn away from evil, which is understanding.

Chapters 29 and 30 are a continuation of Job's discourse. Job looks back on what has been. He reflects on what life was like before this deep suffering came upon him. He longs for the past when he experienced God's presence and felt God's favor and friendship so clearly. He laments the pain and suffering he experienced and reflects on how he desired and hoped for good but has experienced so much evil and brokenness.

As we read through Job's account, we must look to Jesus. Through Him and in Him, we experience the presence and favor of God, even in heartache. The gospel does not preach that as believers all suffering will go away but that in Christ we are never alone. He is always with us.

When we do not know what to do, and when we do not understand what God is doing, we must run to the Lord and His Word. We must trust that His ways and His plans are best, even when they do not make sense to us. We can trust Him and know that true wisdom is found in Him alone.

Reflect on Proverbs 3:5-6, in light of Job 28:23-24. How do these two passages grow your understanding of God's plan and His sovereignty?

Reread Job 29:14. What are some practical ways that you can "put on" righteousness? How does this verse encourage you toward holiness?

Take some time to consider James 1:5. Is wisdom something that you see lacking in your own life? Take a moment in prayer, asking God for His wisdom.

Job 31-33

As Job makes his final appeal to the Lord, the age-old question of why bad things happen to good people presents itself.

Job walked the delicate balance of trusting in the Lord and hoping in the Redeemer while having uncertainty about why he was suffering. But God is sovereign in all things. Though Satan had taken much in this attack and testing of Job, he did not step one inch further than the Lord would allow. We do not always know why God allows us to face suffering in this life, but we know that He will be faithful to us as He works out everything for His glory and our good (Romans 8:28).

Job's appeal to the Lord in chapter 31 also allows us to see a picture of Job's life as he testifies to how he has lived and serves as a reminder to us of Jesus's teaching. Job speaks of loving his neighbor, helping the needy, and even avoiding the love of money. He has lived righteously and very similarly to how Jesus calls His followers to live in the Sermon on the Mount. And though Job lived long before Christ walked the earth, his suffering reminds us of how Christ says in John 16:33 that this world would bring us trouble but to take heart, for He has overcome the world!

In chapters 32 and 33, we hear from a man who has not yet spoken in this narrative. His name is Elihu, and he is much younger than Job and his friends. He has been waiting to speak and is burning with anger against Job. He believes that the purpose of all Job has done is to justify his righteousness when he should be justifying the Lord's righteousness. While Elihu attempts to teach Job, he inadvertently points to his pride and foolishness as he condemns Job, just as the other three friends have done.

However, there exists a poignant part of Elihu's narrative at the end of chapter 33 that is worth noting. Elihu speaks to Job regarding man's need for a mediator to save them from the pit of sin—it is God who perfectly fills that position, delivering man to righteousness when we give our lives to Him. Job 33:22-30 foreshadows what Christ will do on the cross as this mediator to make a way, saving us from the pit of sin and restoring our relationship with God.

In chapter 31, Job examines himself and his life and, in so doing, makes a list of sins. Spend some time in self-examination as we see Job do. Pray that God would reveal to you the sins in your life of which you are unaware.

In chapters 32 and 33, Elihu foolishly boasts in his words and the wisdom he has. Reflect on how you may sometimes come across to your friends. Are you more often like Elihu, proud to speak about what you know, or are you like our Savior, slow to speak and quick to listen?

Which verse about man's need for a mediator stands out to you in Job 33:22-30?

Job 34-36

Elihu continues to narrate these next few chapters, and while the statements he makes of the Lord's character are true — and ones for Job and us to consider — he also continues to accuse Job of untrue things.

Elihu focuses on God's justice and His greatness but does so to highlight that the Lord is giving Job what he deserves, and Job should not question the Lord. However, the danger in what Elihu says is twofold. First, the idea of "Christian karma" is at play here. This is essentially the idea that when we do good, we will receive a blessing, and when we transgress, we will receive punishment. While it is wise to consider the principle that we reap what we sow, the idea of God giving us either blessing or punishment based on our right or wrong actions is not the gospel. If we received what we truly deserved for our actions, all of us would receive eternal punishment for our sin, but God has saved us from ourselves through the atoning work of Jesus on the cross.

The second problem with what Elihu says is that not all suffering is because of our wrongdoing. We indeed live in a fallen world that has been made sick with sin. We feel the effect of the fallen world every day, and some of those effects produce suffering. But while God sovereignly allows some of this suffering to be part of our lives, He does not create evil. The way in which Elihu attributes every situation we face as coming directly from the Lord would eliminate evil itself, for nothing that comes from the Lord's hand is evil. Elihu failed to speak of God's love and mercy, which meant that he gave an incomplete picture of the Lord. We must be careful to learn every aspect of our God to know the fullness of who He is and understand His character.

In Chapter 36, Elihu speaks of the greatness of God because he believes Job has too low a view of God, and while we know that Job does deeply fear the Lord, we can still learn from parts of what Elihu says. In verses 8-10, Elihu explains how the Lord opens the eyes of men who are caught in sin to the truth. He does this so they will serve Him. Any of us who follow Jesus have experienced this. Jesus set us free from the bondages of sin and death, and we can live righteously because He placed His righteousness on us.

We may not understand all that happens to us, but we can trust God's heart. Our God is a God of justice and majesty, but He is also a God of love, grace, and mercy. He does not lead us anywhere He is not.

"We may not understand all that happens to us, but we can trust God's heart."

How does the gospel overrule the idea of "Christian karma"?

Meditate on the characteristics of God that Elihu focuses on in chapter 34. List out the different aspects you find, and spend some time in prayer, asking that God would give you a balanced view of His nature.

In Job 36:24-26, Elihu makes a strong charge to praise God. As you reflect on this verse, in what ways can you be more intentional with your praise and worship of God?

Job 37-39

Chapter 37 is the last part of the story that Job's young friend, Elihu, will narrate.

While Elihu believes that Job's questions and cries to the Lord are evidence of unrepentant sin, he also has beautiful things to say about who God is and what He does. Chapter 37 contains vivid imagery of God controlling the storms, snow, and ice and His voice being in the thunder. Elihu goes on to explain the wondrous works of God and then ends the chapter urging Job to realize how high above man is our God—so high that we cannot reach him. And as Elihu ends his narrative, saying that Job should not be like men "who are wise in heart," because the Almighty is so great that men cannot find him, the Lord does the opposite of what Elihu says. He comes near to Job and speaks out of the whirlwind, a sign of His presence in other parts of Scripture as well (Psalm 77:18, Nahum 1:3, Isaiah 66:15, Ezekiel 1:4). In the same way, God continues to come near to man and dwell with him, even when it requires that He come in the form of a man Himself—in the person of Jesus Christ.

In chapters 38 and 39, the Lord declares to Job who He is by asking Job a series of questions intended to cause Job to pause and wonder. Job had many questions throughout the book, but when God answered from heaven, Job realized that he needed God and not just the answers to his questions. God gave Job just a small glimpse of His majesty and glory, and it would leave Job speechless. God asked Job many questions, but Job did not answer because he did not know the answer. But God was not looking for Job's answers; God was showing Job that He was all-powerful, all-wise, and all-knowing.

We will not always know the answers to the questions this life brings, but ultimately, Christ is the answer. We do not know, but He does. We may not understand, but He does. His plans may not make sense to us, but they have been set forth from the beginning of time. His ways are righteous and sure, and we can trust them because we can trust Him.

These chapters are a beautiful reminder that the great and powerful God who speaks to Job is near to us as well. Though God may never question us in the manner that Job was, He is with us always. Those who believe have been adopted as His sons and daughters because of Christ's work on the cross. Jesus has made it possible for us to call this wondrous Lord our Father.

Chapter 37 begins with a description of God's voice. Does this description remind you of other passages in Scripture? (Revelation 14:2, Psalm 18:13) What characteristics of God are highlighted through this description?

Reread Job 37:14-18, and ask yourself the same questions that Elihu asks Job. Do you find yourself considering the wondrous works of God as you reflect on these things?

Chapters 38-39 are powerful — in what ways do these chapters impact you? Do you find yourself humbled through them?

Job 40-42

After the Lord had spoken and it was Job's turn to speak, Job humbly responds.

When we see who God is, our response should be the same. God is all-powerful, and His plans are never thwarted. He is a good Father, and though we do not always understand His ways, we can trust Him in all things. The Lord continues to speak after Job repents and gives amazing imagery of great beasts He created. The Lord is showing Job that if Job cannot contend with these mighty beasts, what makes him believe that he can contend with their maker, the Lord Almighty? Job is humbled further and asks the Lord to forgive Him. He tells the Lord that He "can do anything" (Job 42:2). The Lord silences Job but also comforts Job by coming near to him.

After the Lord's correction, He turns His attention to Job's friends who did not advise him well but wrongly accused Job of sin he did not commit. The Lord has Job intercede in prayer for his friends as they offer a burnt offering for their folly. In this way, Job represents Jesus, our intercessor. While Job intercedes and shows mercy to the friends who have slandered him, Jesus intercedes for all of the men and women who God has called to Himself.

At the close of the book of Job, the Lord restores all of Job's fortune, and in fact, Job receives double what he had before. Job 42:12 says that God blessed the latter days of Job more than the beginning. Job had even more children and was able to see the lives of many of his descendants before he died, "old and full of days" (Job 42:16). Our God is a God of restoration.

The beginning of this book presents the question: Is the Lord still worthy of worship in our suffering? Job learns that He is—God is worthy of worship for who He is. Even when we do not understand, we can trust Him. Even when we do not understand, we can know that He is good. Even when we do not understand, we can worship Him. He is on our side, and He will surely be faithful.

The same God who came to Job in the whirlwind and was present with him in his suffering is also present with us every moment because Jesus has restored our fellowship to Him. His Spirit lives within us, and we live for His glory through His strength and power.

"We live for His glory through His strength and power."

Reread Job 40:2. In what ways does this verse encourage you to trust the Lord more fully?

In Job 40:4-5 and 42:2-6, we see Job's responses to God. These verses can give us an insight into his humble character. What can you learn about how we should approach God from these verses?

Now that we have finished the book of Job, spend some time reflecting on what you have learned. What are some of the lessons that have impacted your walk with God?

Praise
the Lord.
Hallelujah!

Psalms

GENRE: *Wisdom, Poetry*

AUTHOR / DATE WRITTEN

*Various, including King David, Asaph,
Sons of Korah, and Solomon, among others*

•

*Written over the span of centuries,
likely compiled formally from 537–500 BC*

MAJOR THEMES — *The Future Messiah and His Kingdom,
Meditation and Love of God's Word*

KEY WORDS — *Messiah, Praise, Hallelujah*

KEY VERSE

PSALM 150:6

Let everything that breathes praise the Lord. Hallelujah!

Psalms 1-5

Psalms speaks into just about any situation, and yet praise and adoration of God is the theme repeated throughout this collection of writings.

He is our delight, and we love His law. Psalms 1 and 2 are both written by an anonymous author, and they set up Psalms as a book of prayer for God's covenant people. Psalm 1 encourages the righteous to meditate on God's Word and to abide in the Lord. Abiding in Him is what produces the life of righteousness. Some have even said that Psalm 1 shows us a picture of Jesus, the ultimate righteous One, and then exhorts us to live like Him in contrast to the wickedness found on Earth.

Psalm 2 definitively introduces the Messiah in Psalm 2 as the King who rules over all nations, and the Lord specifically refers to this ruler as His Son. Jesus is the Son of whom this psalm speaks, and He fulfills the covenant God made with David that would establish His throne forever (2 Samuel 7:8-16). Thus, Psalms 1 and 2 encourage the covenant people of God to love the Word of God and to look forward to the day the Messiah will reign.

David is the author of Psalms 3-5. In Psalm 3, David cries to the Lord that He is David's salvation and shield as he flees from his son, Absalom, who is trying to kill him. However, Jesus also fulfills this psalm as He delivers His people on the "holy hill," Golgotha, when He dies on the cross for our sins. David acknowledges that the Lord is the one who saves him from his enemies, and in Jesus, we are also saved from our enemies: sin and death.

In Psalm 4, which is often known as the "Evening Prayer," David calls the Lord a "God, who vindicates," freeing him from affliction and giving joy and peace. We can rest in Him as we lie down in sleep as we trust His good and perfect character. Similarly, Jesus calls us to rest in Him as He is "lowly and humble in heart" (Matthew 11:29).

Psalm 5 contains an urgent and expectant prayer from David as he seeks refuge from his enemies. He says to the Lord that He will enter His house only because of the Lord's steadfast love. This reminds us that we do not have access to an intimate relationship with the Lord because of anything we have done but because of the love the Lord has first demonstrated to us through Christ.

"We can rest in Him as we lie down in sleep as we trust His good and perfect character."

Though we cannot study each psalm in depth in this study, let each one continually remind you of who the Lord is and all that He has done for us. The Psalms contain many heartfelt, anguished cries of covenant people to their faithful King. This reminds us that life will not always be easy, but He will always be with us.

How does Psalm 1 remind you of the righteousness of Christ?

Reflect on Psalm 4:8. How does this verse comfort you by reminding you of the security we have in God?

Pick a psalm from the reading today, and take a moment to read through the words in prayer to God.

Psalms 6-10

A Penitential Psalm is a song of humble repentance and confession to the Lord for sin. David is deeply distressed and looking to God for help. He does not know if his trouble comes from God because of sin in his life or if it results from the wickedness of his enemies. Regardless, he seeks the Lord and knows that the Lord hears his cry. Because we now belong to Christ, Jesus has become our intercessor (Hebrews 7:25). When we experience trouble as David did, we can call out to Jesus, knowing that He identifies with us in our suffering and will never forsake us (Hebrews 4:15, Hebrews 13:5).

Psalm 7 continues in the theme of Psalm 6 with the topic of suffering. It contains a song David writes after a Benjamite man wrongly accuses him. This psalm reminds us that as believers of Jesus, we will certainly suffer and experience rejection from the world as our Savior did so long ago. But like David, we can depend on the Lord in all of our sufferings because He is righteous and true. Our identity is not in the words of others but in the righteousness the Lord has placed on us because of Christ's work on the cross.

Psalm 8 is a beautiful depiction of the redemptive story of the Bible. David begins the psalm by addressing God as "Lord, our Lord" and then declaring His glorious creation of the heavens. However, in verse 2, we see that God has foes and enemies in the world. This serves as a reminder that even though the glory of God surrounds us, the world is under the curse of sin because of the fall. And while humanity lives in this fallen world, God still allows us to be stewards of His creation. Because of the gospel, He restores us to Himself. Psalm 8:6-8 ultimately gives us a picture of Christ Himself, the One to whom everything in creation is subjected because all things were made "through Him and for Him" (Colossians 1:16). The end of Psalm 8 repeats the beginning, and it gives a picture of the final restoration of the world, where all creation will sing of the majesty of the Lord. Someday, all things will be made right, and the curse will be no more (Revelation 22:3).

Psalms 9 and 10 are companion psalms highlighting the Lord as the King who will reign forever, war against the wicked, and save the oppressed (Psalm

"Our great King sees this evil and will not let it go unanswered."

142

9:7-10, Psalm 10:16-18). In this world, believers will be faced with evil and brokenness, but our great King sees this evil and will not let it go unanswered. As subjects of Jesus, we imitate Him in serving the helpless and needy, knowing that we too were once in need of grace and mercy that He so lovingly bestowed upon us.

QUESTIONS

Meditate on Psalm 8:3-4. In what ways does this passage grow your understanding of God's love for us?

Reread Psalm 9:9-10. How do these verses encourage you to rely on the Lord and continue seeking Him?

Psalm 10 begins with a question to which we can all likely relate in sympathy, but it ends with confidence in the Lord. How can this psalm impact the way you respond in times of suffering and confusion?

Psalms 11-15

In Psalm 11, David is likely fleeing from Saul, who was seeking to take his life.

This psalm is a song of confidence in the Lord despite David's circumstances. Likewise, believers can find their confidence in knowing that Jesus is our refuge. When our enemies destroy our foundations, the Lord is not passive. He will actively attend to our needs, even if it seems as if the wicked do not receive justice. Vindication for all evildoing is coming when Christ returns; however, those who love Him "shall behold his face" (Psalm 11:7).

We find David overwhelmed in Psalm 12 by the lack of godly men in leadership around him—an abundance of men who lie, cover their sin, and oppress the needy. The Lord watches over the poor and oppressed, and He comes to their rescue. In this psalm, we can see the heart of Christ. Our Savior spent much of His earthly ministry with the people the world so often forgets and mistreats, even today. Yet, we can find comfort in the Lord's covenant love to His people from generation to generation.

Throughout the Psalms, David often wrestles with what he feels and knows to be true of the Lord. Our hearts and emotions often deceive us (Jeremiah 17:9), but the Lord's character never changes. Psalm 13 is an example of this struggle. However, the last two verses of Psalm 13 are brought to their ultimate fulfillment in Christ. Our hearts trust in the steadfast love of the Lord and rejoice in His salvation—salvation made possible because of Christ's work on the cross. We can also sing like David to the Lord, for He has treated us graciously (Psalm 13:6). Truly, those who are in Christ have a beautiful inheritance (1 Peter 1:4).

Psalm 14 shows a picture of practical atheism. The foolish say in their hearts that there is no God, and unfortunately, all men are prone to live as if this were true. We think that we know what is best for ourselves, and we often exalt ourselves to the place of God in our hearts and lives. But the Lord saves us from our sinful hearts. We do not naturally seek the Lord, but praise God that He sought us and loved us first (1 John 4:19, Romans 5:8).

"Only through Him can we be righteous and dwell with God."

Psalm 15 was likely written after the ark of the covenant was returned to Jerusalem. In this psalm, David seeks the Lord and longs to walk in a relationship with Him. In answer to the question that asks who can dwell with the Lord, the answer given here is, "The one who lives blamelessly, practices righteousness, and acknowledges the truth in his heart" (Psalm 15:2). This again points to Jesus, the only one who is truly blameless. Only through Him can we be righteous and dwell with God (Ephesians 2:19).

QUESTIONS

In what ways does Psalm 13 encourage you to dwell on what is true?
What are some practical steps you can take to carry this out?

How does Psalm 15 give examples of how we should live?
How does this make you grateful for Christ's holiness?

Choose a psalm to reflect on in-depth. Spend some time in prayer,
reading the psalm as you pray.

Psalms 16-20

Psalm 16 is a psalm of joy in the Lord. Our joy is not dependent on our circumstances but on who He is.

And in Him, we have "a beautiful inheritance" (Psalm 16:6). This psalm ultimately points us to the gospel and is later quoted by Peter as he shows how Christ fulfills it (Acts 2:25-33). The Lord, who was at David's right hand, came to be with the world in the person of Jesus Christ. Our hearts can be glad, and we can rejoice like David because we are secure through the work of our Savior (Psalm 16:9)! Someday we will be with Jesus at His right hand, and there will be no end to the joys of standing in His presence (Ephesians 2:6, Psalm 16:11)!

In Psalm 17, David looks for vindication from the Lord as he flees from his enemies. David is confident that when he cries out to the Lord, He will answer. In verses 6 and 7, we find the heart of this psalm and a picture of what believers have in Christ. We call upon the Lord, and He answers us. The Lord has shown His steadfast love to us by sending Jesus, who has become our rock and refuge. Jesus has saved us from the adversaries of sin and death, so we shall one day behold His face, for we are covered in His righteousness (Psalm 17:15).

Psalm 18 shows us how God hears the prayers of His people and acts on our behalf. Psalm 18:19 reminds us that He has rescued us because of His steadfast love for us. He does not rescue us out of obligation but because He delights in us. And after He saves us, He equips us to walk in His strength and salvation (Psalm 18:31-36).

Psalm 19 shows us how God makes Himself known in creation, His Word, and our hearts. The heavens show His glory, and His Word shows us who He is. But in His creation alone, God has given every person an opportunity to turn to Him for salvation. The Word of God shines the truth of the majesty we see around us: the Lord is God, and He has created all things. It also exposes our sinful hearts and need for Him and His righteousness—righteousness we can only possess in Christ.

Psalm 20 contains other people's prayers for David before he goes into battle, but many scholars have also viewed this as a prophetic prayer of Jesus before

"The heavens show His glory, and His Word shows us who He is."

His battle with sin and death on the cross. As children of God, we can call on the One who helped David and who strengthened Jesus. He always answers the call of His people. His faithfulness is on display in the entire story of Scripture, and it continues today in our daily walk with Him.

QUESTIONS

Reread Psalm 16:5-11. What does this verse tell you about the joy and delight we have in Christ?

Meditate on Psalm 18:19. In what ways does this verse expand your understanding of who God is? How does this verse grow your confidence in Him?

What does Psalm 19:7-8 show you about loving the instruction of the Lord?

Psalms 21-25

Psalm 20 is a prayer for victory in battle, and
Psalm 21 is a song of praise following that
glorious victory.

While David is the king, the people describe Jesus as the final fulfillment of its words. Jesus, like David, rejoices in the Lord's strength and exults in the Lord's salvation (Psalm 21:1). The Lord has bestowed splendor and majesty on Him, and Jesus is glad in the presence of His Father (Psalm 21:5-6). A day is also coming when the Lord will defeat all of His enemies (Psalm 21:9).

While Psalm 22 was first written to describe the suffering of David, it prophetically describes the death of Christ on the cross. The first words of this psalm are the very words Jesus cries out to His Heavenly Father as He bore God's wrath for sin: "My God, my God, why have you abandoned me?" Here in this psalm, we see our Messiah suffer so that His friends and followers could enter into fellowship with God. The psalm ends with God's promise to Israel that is fulfilled in salvation through Jesus: "All the ends of the earth will remember and turn to the Lord. And all the families of the nations will bow down before you" (Psalm 22:27).

The familiarity of Psalm 23, one of the most well-known passages in Scripture, does not diminish its beauty. Throughout all of Scripture, we see descriptions of the Lord as our Shepherd (Genesis 48:15, 49:24, Psalm 28:9, 80:1, 95:7, 100:3). When God comes to earth in the person of Jesus, He also describes Himself as the Good Shepherd (John 10:11). Jesus watches after the redeemed and is intimately involved with the joys and struggles of our lives. We find everything we need in Him.

We read Psalm 24 as a triumphant song of the King of Glory. David likely wrote this psalm when the ark of the covenant returned to Jerusalem (2 Samuel 6, 1 Chronicles 15:1-16:3). He begins with the declaration that the earth is the Lord's, and then David asks, "Who may ascend the mountain of the Lord?" (Psalm 24:3) David writes that it is only "the one who has clean hands and a pure heart" (Psalm 24:4). No man inherently possesses these qualities except Christ, but by His life, death, and resurrection, all men can obtain them. We can ascend the hill of the Lord and be in His presence because Christ has given us clean hands and a pure heart by His righteousness.

"We can have friendship with God and trust in Him as our refuge forever."

Psalm 25 is a passionate plea from the heart of David to the Lord not to let him be put to shame. And because of the Lord's steadfast love and forgiveness for His people, none who put their trust in Him will ever be put to shame. Psalm 25 puts the gospel on display. The Lord instructs sinners in the way of truth and pardons our guilt, not because of our worthiness but because of His steadfast love. We can have friendship with God and trust in Him as our refuge forever.

QUESTIONS

List another way that Psalm 21 is fulfilled in Christ, other than what was mentioned in today's reading.

Reread Psalm 22, and pause to remember Christ's sacrifice on the cross. As you read, imagine Jesus saying these words, and pray a prayer of gratitude for our Savior and His love for His people.

How does your perspective change regarding your present-day situations when you know of the Lord's goodness to those who fear Him and obey His commands?

Psalms 26-30

While he has walked in integrity, David knows that it is only because of the Lord's steadfast love (Psalm 26:1-3). David is not boasting of his good works in this psalm. Rather, he cries out for God's strength in his pursuit of holiness. We, like David, do not naturally possess holiness. It is only by the grace of God through Jesus that we are not swept away with sinners as Psalm 26 describes (Ephesians 2:8-9) but find our home in Christ (John 14:23).

Psalm 27 reminds us that the presence of the Lord is all that we need. David calls the Lord his light, salvation, stronghold, and shelter. When we know who the Lord is and that He is with us, we will not be afraid, and He will give us His courage. God has sought to be present with His people since the beginning of the story of redemption! In David's time, God was present in the tabernacle, but one day soon, He would be present in His Son, Jesus. We now possess His very presence through the Holy Spirit! And we wait with strength and courage (Psalm 27:14) for the new life to come, for when Christ returns, we will see His goodness and remain in His presence forevermore.

In Psalm 28, David cries out and pleads with the Lord to hear him and be faithful to him. He begs God not to be silent toward his pleas (Psalm 28:1). And at the end of this psalm, David reminds himself of who God is. The Lord is David's strength and shield, and He has promised David that His throne would be established forever (2 Samuel 7:13). Jesus will fulfill this promise to David as the great and final King who will reign forever. And as we read at the end of this psalm, Jesus will be our Shepherd, and He will carry us until the very end (Psalm 28:9, Matthew 28:20).

David refers to "the Lord" eighteen times in Psalm 29 as he describes Israel's covenant God. He uses imagery to show the Lord's glory and strength. He is God over the waters and thunder. His voice is powerful and can break the "cedars of Lebanon" and call forth fire (Psalm 29:5, 7). Jesus shows Himself to be God by commanding the waters and storms to obey Him. As His disciples frantically scrambled around their boat in the midst of a storm, thinking they would certainly perish, Jesus brought everything to peace (Mark 4:35-41). And in the same way, the Lord's glory and strength, as described in Psalm 29, gives His people peace in their troubles (Psalm 29:11).

"God has healed us and restored us to life through Christ."

Psalm 30 is a song that David prophetically wrote before his son, Solomon, built the temple, but it was sung at the temple's dedication. All that David says of God in this psalm reminds us of the gospel. God has healed us and restored us to life through Christ (Psalm 30:2-3). On the cross, Jesus bore God's wrath for our sin, and His suffering won His followers' favor forever with God. And though all looked lost as Christ took His final breath, joy came in His resurrection (Psalm 30:5). He assuredly turns our mourning into dancing!

QUESTIONS

How does Psalm 27:1 give you confidence in the Lord? How does confidence in the Lord affect our willingness to wait on Him (as described in Psalm 27:14)?

Reread Psalm 28:1. Do you find yourself calling on the Lord as your first reaction to trouble? How does reading through this psalm encourage you to do so?

Reread Psalm 30:11-12. Recall a time in your life when God took something full of mourning and turned it into joy.

Psalms 31-35

Psalm 31 contains the very words Jesus cried as He gave His last breath on the cross (Luke 23:46): "Into your hand I entrust my spirit" (Psalm 31:5).

"Because we are in Christ, we can trust that He will rescue us from all of our fears."

Because of His life, death, and resurrection, we can cry these words, as well as the words that follow: "You have redeemed me, Lord, God of truth" (Psalm 31:5). We can commit ourselves entirely to Him, for He has redeemed us by the blood of His Son, and we can trust in His steadfast love forever. The fear and overwhelming situations we may face will not consume us because of the steadfast love of the Lord and the abundant goodness He has stored up for those who fear Him (Psalm 31:19).

Psalm 32 describes how those who are forgiven are blessed. Forgiveness of sin requires the shedding of blood. Our transgressions have been forgiven, and our sins have been covered by the blood of Jesus (Romans 3:21-26). This is known as the doctrine of propitiation in which Christ was the atoning sacrifice for us on the cross. Because He shed His blood for us, we no longer need to cover our sin through the sacrificial system as David did. Christ's sacrifice was enough. And because we have salvation in Him, righteousness and joy are ours forevermore (Psalm 32:11)!

Psalm 33:1 continues with a call for the righteous to rejoice in the Lord. Praise befits the people of God. The psalm describes the Lord as trustworthy in all His work and loving righteousness and justice (Psalm 33:4-5). Righteousness and justice do not characterize the world, but regardless, the Lord has filled the earth with His steadfast love! He allows us to live and know Him! And once we learn to fear God, His eyes never leave us (Psalm 33:18). He freely welcomes us into His kingdom.

When David flees from Saul into the territory of the Philistines, He comes to the city of Gath and is presented to King Achish, or Abimelech, as Psalm 34 describes. David pretends to be mad so that he can escape, for the Philistines would have taken great joy in putting him to death. Goliath, the giant whom David famously defeated, was from Gath. David had also killed many Philistines since coming into the service of Saul. This was a close call for David, and Psalm 34 shows Him praising the Lord. David knows the Lord has always been with him, even in the most dangerous situations, and so it is for us. Because we are in Christ, we can trust that He will rescue us from all of our fears (Psalm 34:4).

Psalm 35 is an Imprecatory Psalm. These can be difficult to read as Imprecatory Psalms are for the cursing of enemies, yet they remind us that the world will stand against us; Jesus promised it (John 15:18-19). Under the new covenant, we are called to pray for our enemies rather than curse them (Matthew 5:44). Our hope is that our enemies will be restored to Christ and that our trust in God will soften their hearts to the truth of who He is (Psalm 35:27).

QUESTIONS

Reread Psalm 31:19. Reflect on what it means to "fear" the Lord and take "refuge" in Him. Do you think that displaying these qualities comes easily to you? How does this verse encourage you to grow in these areas?

How does Psalm 34:4-5 grow your confidence in the Lord? Do you truly believe that He will answer your prayers and deliver you from fear?

In what ways does Psalm 35 teach you to praise God and have joy and delight in Him?

Psalms 36-40

David begins Psalm 36 with a description of
a wicked man.

This wicked man has no fear of God, and because of this, he proudly believes that no one will ever find out about his sin. He speaks only deceitful things and does no good. Upon closer look, we realize that we were all once this type of wicked man. And only God can save us from our sin, which is why David goes on to declare the great and merciful attributes of God in verse 5. There is so much available to us in the Lord when we are in Christ. And it is not because of our works but because of His steadfast love toward us (Psalm 36:5-10).

Psalm 37 reminds us that God will never forsake His people, even when it seems like the wicked are prospering and God's people are not. This psalm is full of commands to the believer: to trust in the Lord, delight in the Lord, commit your way to the Lord, and wait silently before the Lord (Psalm 37:3-7). David is encouraging the people to look to the Lord and the future that is coming! They do not need to worry about the wicked in the present day. God's people will inherit the land, God's eternal country, and live there forever (Psalm 37:29). Because we have put our trust in Christ, we will live forever with our great King!

Psalm 38 is the third of the Penitential Psalms of David. You may remember from Psalm 6 that a Penitential Psalm is a song of humble repentance and confession to the Lord for sin. David felt the weight of God's discipline, and he was broken by it. He was also deeply discouraged by his companions' rejection of him because of his sin and his enemies' rejoicing over his failure. When David put all of his focus on the people around him, he was distraught. When his attention went to the Lord, he found hope. When our sin feels too heavy and overwhelming, we can go to the cross and draw near to our Savior. He has redeemed us, and He will restore us.

David begins Psalm 39 by again focusing on his sin, which leads him to ponder the brevity of human life. Suffering in this world reminds us that our lives here are fleeting. If we become too attached to this world, we are sure to be quickly reminded that this is not our true home. And in light of how we struggle with the presence of sin in this world, that is good news. Our struggle will not be forever. We are only sojourners here but permanent residents of the kingdom of God whose king is Christ.

"Jesus was the embodiment of the Lord's constant love and salvation."

Psalm 40 relates to the life of David, but it is also a messianic Psalm—which means that it is about Jesus—and is quoted by Jesus in Hebrews 10:5-9. Jesus came and revealed what was written about Himself in the Old Testament (Psalm 40:7). He delighted to do the will of God, and He delivered the news of deliverance to the people (Psalm 40:8-9). Jesus was the embodiment of the Lord's constant love and salvation (Psalm 40:10). Because of what Christ has done, we can join with the psalmist and those who love salvation by saying, "The Lord is great!" (Psalm 40:16).

QUESTIONS

Focus on chapter 36 for a moment, and look up the definition for the word "steadfast." How does this word grow your understanding of God's love?

Meditate on Psalm 38:15. How does this verse encourage you to wait on the Lord and trust His timing?

In Psalm 39:4, we see David plead to God that He would let him "know how short-lived" he is. Why do you think that this is such an important plea?

Psalms 41-45

The first book of Psalms draws to a close in Psalm 41.
The beatitude, or blessing, in verse 1 explains that those
who consider the poor are blessed.

Whenever a believer cares deeply for marginalized or outcasts, that person reflects the heart of Jesus, who spent much of His earthly ministry with people the world so often overlooked (Isaiah 61:1). David trusts in the Lord's blessing, even when his enemies tried to conspire against him. We could insert Jesus into David's situation. Religious leaders of David's day also conspired against him, just as Jesus's close friend, Judas, betrayed Him (Psalm 41:7,9). However, in verses 10-11, we see that, like Jesus, God does not allow David's enemies to shout in triumph over him.

Psalms 42 and 43 begin the second collection of Psalms, and they are both connected by the theme of spiritual depression. The psalmist was troubled, and he thirsted for God like a deer pants for water. The Lord is the one for whom we thirst, and He is the one who has redeemed us. He is our sustenance and the desire of our souls. In the same way that we desire physical food and drink, we should desire the Lord and His presence. Jesus is living water and the Bread of Life, and He will satisfy every hunger and thirst of our souls when we come to Him (John 4:13-14, John 6:35). Even though we may sometimes feel like God has rejected us because He seems distant and far off, this is never the case (Psalm 43:2). Once we are in Christ, the Lord will never reject us (Romans 8:38-39).

Psalm 44 is a prayer of praise and honest petition. The psalmist begins by recalling Israel's spiritual legacy, which we know will ultimately be fulfilled in Christ, the promised Messiah. The first few verses are a beautiful display of God's eternal plan for His people, but the verses that follow show the people in deep distress. The psalmist claims that God has rejected them by allowing their enemies to repeatedly defeat them. The psalmist questions God's purposes, and this can serve as a reminder to us that we also can come before the Lord with honest questions. He desires our fellowship with Himself, and when we come to Him, He will hear us.

We can read Psalm 45 and know that it points to Jesus, the messianic King who will be blessed forever and whose name will be remembered from generation

"The Lord is the one for whom we thirs, and He is the one who has redeemed us."

156

to generation (Psalm 45:2, 17). And His church is His bride, the princess in "clothing embroidered with gold" (Psalm 45:13). As the psalm describes a king's bride being led to Him, we are given a glimpse of a future reality that we will one day behold. The Church, Christ's bride, will one day be reunited with her heavenly King, and she will praise Him forever.

—————— QUESTIONS ——————

Read John 4:13-14 and 6:35. How does the knowledge of these two verses help you understand the significance of Psalm 42:1-2?

Reflect on Psalm 43:3. What does it mean to let God's light and truth lead us?

Psalm 45 focuses on the royalty of Christ. Write a response about what you think it will be like to reunite with your heavenly King.

Psalms 46-50

When we look at Psalm 46, we see that it is fulfilled in Jesus. Jesus is Immanuel: "God with us."

We find our refuge and security in Him, and we know He will always be with us until the very end of time (Psalm 46:1, Matthew 28:20). This psalm also points to the eternal city of God where Jesus will reign forever (Psalm 46:4-5). After all of the kingdoms of the earth fall away, only the kingdom of God will remain. God is with us now, but we will physically be in His presence in the life to come. What a hope we have because of Jesus!

Psalm 47 builds on the theme of Psalm 46 by encouraging the people of Israel to rejoice in their King because of the security they have in Him. This psalm is notably directed to all people (Psalm 47:1). The Lord will be King over all the earth (Psalm 47:2). This is the fulfillment of God's promise to Abraham that his offspring would be a blessing to all nations (Genesis 22:18). The people of Israel were messengers of the Lord's greatness to the people around them, and now His church today includes believers from all different tribes, tongues, and nations. While the psalmist is speaking of the city of Jerusalem in Psalm 48, his words can also be applied to the future New Jerusalem where God will be with His people (Revelation 21:2).

Psalm 49 gives us an eternal perspective of riches. We do not need to envy those who are prosperous, for our reward is in heaven. It is not wrong to be wealthy, but it is wrong to put all of your trust in your earthly possessions rather than the Lord. When we pass away, our earthly riches will have no meaning. They also cannot give us the one thing we all need—salvation. Jesus is the only one who can offer Himself as a ransom for our life and save us from the power of hell.

Psalm 50 opens with three names of God: "The Mighty One, God, the Lord" (translated in Hebrew as as *El Elohim Yahweh*). These names show Israel that God is both almighty and personal. He is the covenant God of His people. God reminds His people that He does not need or rely on their sacrifices, for He owns everything that roams the earth (Psalm 50:10). He desires thankfulness, obedience, and prayer. Most of all, He wants their hearts to be for Him alone. Once we are saved in Christ, we do not obey the Lord to earn our salvation out of obligation. We obey Him and offer up ourselves as an offering out of love for our good and perfect Father.

"We obey Him and offer up ourselves as an offering out of love for our good and perfect Father."

Meditate on Psalm 46:10, and take a moment to be still in prayer before God, asking that He would give you a continually deeper understanding of how to "stop your fighting" and be still before Him.

Reread Psalm 49:5. How does this psalm encourage you not to fear in times of trouble but instead trust in God?

Having read Psalm 50, how can you offer God a sacrifice of thanksgiving?

Psalms 51-55

Psalm 51 contains David's cry for forgiveness after Nathan, the prophet, confronts him for his sin of raping Bathsheba and murdering her husband (2 Samuel 12:1-25).

David's actions drove him to misery and separation from God, and he desperately needed the Lord to cleanse and restore him. The depth of our sin is just as great as David's, yet God has shown us compassion and steadfast love by sending Christ to wipe away our transgressions. He reaches into the depths of our dark hearts and creates a new heart filled with His truth and a desire for Him.

One of the most heartbreaking stories in the Bible is when Saul commands Doeg the Edomite to kill Ahimelech and all of the priests of Nob because they helped David as he fled from Saul (1 Samuel 21-22). Doeg killed not only the men but also their wives, children, and animals. And what a seemingly cowardly crime it was. Doeg killed innocent people who were servants of the Lord and had never learned to use a sword—all of because he "trusted in the abundance of his riches" (Psalm 52:7). David condemns Doeg's evil deeds in Psalm 52, and he reminds himself that committing evil for the sake of wealth will only lead to destruction, but trusting in the steadfast love of the Lord will lead to life forever.

Psalm 53 repeats many of the ideas we find in Psalm 14. David again states that those who say in their heart that there is no God are fools, but before we can gladly pat ourselves on the back because we do believe in God, David reminds us that no one does any good thing. Apart from Christ, we would still be hopelessly dead in our sin, and those who remain apart from Christ when He returns to the earth will face destruction. But praise be to God for the gift of salvation!

Psalm 54 is David's response to the betrayal of the Ziphites. The Ziphites were also Israeli and came from the same tribe as David (Judah), yet they tried to help Saul kill David. David models for us that even in the most painful rejection and treachery, we can place our hope in God. While men may try and wrongly come against us, all evil will not go unnoticed by the Lord, and He will surely uphold us. Christ triumphed over our great enemies, sin and death, on the cross, and our hope in eternal life with Him will help us bear the evil that comes our way.

Psalm 55 continues with the theme of Psalm 54—trusting God even in the betrayal of a close companion. Again, the hope of the gospel ensures that

"We do not need to fear."

we will never be moved by the harm that others bring against us in this life. We do not need to fear. God asks us to "cast our burdens" on Him, and He will be our strength. Jesus Himself took on our burden of sin so we that could be made righteous, and He will "never allow the righteous to be shaken" (Psalm 55:22).

QUESTIONS

2 Samuel 11 tells the story of David and Bathsheeba, the incident referenced in David's writing of Psalm 51. How does knowing the backdrop of this psalm shape your perspective of it?

Reread Psalm 54:7. In what ways does this verse grow your confidence in the Lord and His plan?

Psalm 55:22 is a call to cast our burdens on the Lord. After reflecting on this verse, spend some time in prayer, giving your burdens to God and asking Him to sustain you.

Psalms 56-60

Psalm 56 is David's response to the Philistines seizing him in Gath (1 Samuel 21:10-15). As we see David repeatedly remind Himself to trust God, we are reminded to have a right response to our own fears. In light of eternity and Jesus, who is our King, what can man do to us? Man can only destroy our bodies but has no authority over our souls. Christ has delivered our souls from death! We now have fellowship with God and walk with Him "in the light of life" (Psalm 56:13).

When David flees from Saul, one of the places he finds himself is the cave of Adullam (1 Samuel 22:1). David was in a vulnerable position in the cave but saw his situation with eyes of faith. He was in the shadow of the Lord's wing. In Psalm 57, David declares that the Lord is his refuge. God's glory is seen over all the earth as He shows steadfast love, mercy, and faithfulness to people who are not worthy of it. Followers of Christ are hidden, like David, in the shadow of the Lord's wing, and because God has saved His people, His name will be exalted over all the earth.

In Psalm 58, David laments the unjust leaders of the world. This psalm is heavy for us to read, but it is not about revenge. It is about a desire for justice and good to conquer evil. David's words remind us not to become comfortable with sin or used for evil. Instead, we should be saddened by the results of the fall and filled with gratitude for what God has done through Christ. We await the day when evil will be defeated, and we will see our Savior face to face.

David wrote Psalm 59 while running for his life from Saul's men who were trying to kill him. David faces one dangerous situation after another, and in each one, the Lord displays His faithfulness as He delivers David from evil. God is His shield, and through David's temporary suffering, God's name is made great throughout the earth as He destroys the enemies of David. We may face suffering in this life, but God will always be our shield. He will use each instance of suffering and wickedness brought against us to ultimately point to the glory of His name because He is our deliverer.

As we see David erupt with accusations against God in Psalm 60, may our hearts be encouraged that God allows us to come before Him in our honesty,

"We may face suffering in this life, but God will always be our shield."

anger, and confusion. But we are also reminded that we must not remain in our frustration but rest in God's sovereignty. David reminds himself of God's redemptive plan to establish David's throne forever, for the tribe of Judah would have the scepter (Genesis 49:10). Jesus is the final fulfillment of this promise.

QUESTIONS

Focus on Psalm 56:4. Is it easy for you to have this same posture of fearlessness and trust in the Lord? Why or why not?

How does reading Psalm 57 cause your affections for God to grow?

In Psalm 59:17, we see David call God his strength. What does it look like to believe that God is your strength? How does this perspective change the way you live?

Psalms 61-65

In Psalm 61, David models to the people how to pray for their king.

This is important because if Israel's king faithfully upheld their covenant to God, the people would also be blessed (Deuteronomy 17:18-20). David knew he was limited and needed the "rock that is high above me" (Psalm 61:2). At the end of his prayer, David asks that the king remain on the throne forever (Psalm 61:7). David knows he will one day pass away, but he is asking the Lord to fulfill the covenant He made with him by providing a messianic king. Jesus fulfills this prayer.

The Hebrew word for "alone" or "only" repeats itself six times in Psalm 62. David emphasizes that the Lord alone is where we can find hope and salvation. We do not need to anxiously wait for Him to act because we know He is faithful, and we can trust Him. David does not know that it will be many years before the ultimate fulfillment of salvation will arrive through Jesus. And for many years, in trial and difficulty, the Israelites will have to wait on the Lord. And while we know more than they did then, we still have unknowns. We do not know when Christ will return, but we wait and trust in Him alone. Our hope is set in the salvation of the Lord.

Psalm 63 paints a vivid picture of the glory of God, the beauty of His steadfast love, and our ever-present need for Him. David earnestly seeks the Lord so much that He thirsts and faints for Him (Psalm 63:1). This language is similar to what Jesus says in the Sermon on the Mount about how those who hunger and thirst for righteousness will be blessed (Matthew 5:6). The Lord is our satisfaction, and because of His steadfast love for us, we can hope and rest in Christ. His love is truly better than life itself because His love has provided us eternal life with Him forever!

Psalm 64 comments on the power of the tongue. David compares the tongues of the wicked to swords and arrows used against the blameless and goes on to say that though wicked men think their sin is hidden, God sees all and will bring them to ruin because of their actions. This reminds us that any hidden sin in our life is not truly hidden. The Lord sees it, and it will eventually reveal itself. When we face suffering from the hands of those who do not know God, we share in Christ's sufferings and find comfort from His nearness. God will act against evil committed against His people.

"In every facet of creation, we see the Lord, and we know that all we see was made through Christ."

Psalm 65 contains a stunning song of praise. Those who the Lord chooses to bring near are those whose transgressions He has forgiven. Yet He hears them and lets them be in His presence! In every facet of creation, we see the Lord, and we know that all we see was made through Christ. And while we marvel now at the work of the Creator, we will marvel all the more when Christ returns to restore all things to Himself!

QUESTIONS

In Psalm 62:1, David says that he waits for God in silence (ESV). Why do you think it is significant to wait quietly or in silence on the Lord? In what ways can silence benefit our walks with God?

Reread Psalm 63:8. Do you find that your soul clings to God? In what ways does this psalm teach us to hold fast to our heavenly Father?

At the beginning of Psalm 65, we see that praise is rightfully the Lord's. Why might this be significant?

Through Israel's worship of the Lord, the other nations would be blessed, and they would see a picture of the heavenly kingdom that is coming—one where they could belong as citizens! God preserved the nation of Israel because of His steadfast love for them and because He would bring the Messiah from their line. God has been faithful, and we are part of the people of the nations, drawn into a new covenant with a faithful God!

Some of the words of the Aaronic blessing begin Psalm 67, but instead of being only for the people of Israel, the blessing found in Numbers 6:22-27 extends to the entire earth. God's graciousness to Israel will cause the nations to follow Him—they will know of the saving power of His salvation (Psalm 67:2), seen through the work of Christ! The Lord repeatedly shows that while Israel is His covenant people, He seeks to use them to draw all people to Himself.

Many commentators believe that Psalm 68 is about the ark of the covenant arriving in Jerusalem (2 Samuel 6). This event shows God's power over Israel's enemies and His preservation of His people. David uses this psalm to provide a record of the Lord's faithfulness, but it also points to how He will deliver them in the future (Psalm 68:19-20). The Lord will deliver His people from death through Jesus and provide eternal salvation.

Psalm 69 is filled with deep sorrow and grief as the psalmist cries out for rescue. His suffering, in fact, ultimately points to Christ's suffering on the cross. Like David, who sinks into the mire of trouble, Jesus sinks into the mire of humanity's sin (Psalm 69:2). David was hated by many without cause, though he was a king after God's own heart. Jesus taught that this verse was fulfilled in Himself, and He was God in flesh (John 15:25). David and Jesus both also have a zeal for the house of God (2 Samuel 7:1-3, John 2:17). And Psalm 69:21 is ultimately fulfilled as Jesus is given vinegar to drink on the cross (John 19:28-29). But what is strikingly different about David and Jesus in this psalm is that while David prays against his enemies, Jesus prays for His enemies. Jesus forgives His enemies as He is on the cross (Psalm 69:22-28, Luke 23:34). While we were once enemies of God, God pursued us and opened our eyes to salvation (Colossians 1:21-22). We are forgiven.

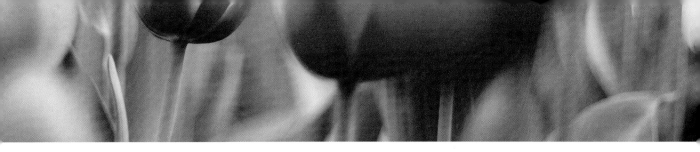

The language of Psalm 70 is very similar to Psalm 40, but David seems more urgent and hard-pressed as he prays to God. David asks the Lord twice to make haste to help him (Psalm 70:1,5). You can almost imagine David running as he cries these words out to God, but he knows that God is his deliverer. David is "needy" on his own, and so are we (Psalm 70:5). We need salvation and deliverance through Jesus. As believers, we can cry out to Him for help, knowing that He is always with us.

QUESTIONS

Reread Psalm 66:16. What has God done for you that you need to proclaim to others?

Highlight all the ways that Psalm 69 points you to Jesus. Which way sticks out to you most?

Meditate on one of the psalms from today's reading. Take a moment to pray through the psalm to the Lord.

Psalms 71-75

And though we grey and our skin wrinkles, our hope is in the Lord and not in our youth. He is the one who never changes and will be with us until the very end. The psalmist foreshadows the resurrection, declaring that the Lord would raise him up from "the depths of the earth" (Psalm 71:20). Death, the last enemy, will not threaten our souls because Jesus has power over it through His death and resurrection.

Psalm 72 is the first psalm attributed to Solomon, and though the psalm describes his kingship, the kingship is ultimately fulfilled by the coming of Jesus, the King of kings. Jesus is the only perfect King, and He rules with complete righteousness and peace. His dominion will be even greater than Solomon's, and He will have dominion from "sea to sea" (Psalm 72:8). Jesus's Kingdom will endure forever, and He will bless all peoples of the earth, thus fulfilling the covenants the Lord made with David and Abraham (Psalm 72:17, 2 Samuel 7:12-13, Genesis 12:1-3).

Psalm 73 begins the third book of Psalms, and it is the first psalm written by Asaph, a great musician during the era of David and Solomon. Asaph declares the goodness of God but then explains his struggle with seeing the wicked flourish. Even though we will not always see justice immediately carried out, we can rest assured that Jesus will bring it to pass when He returns. Asaph comes to the Lord with his frustration and doubt, but as soon as he is in the Lord's presence in the sanctuary, he repents and is reminded that God is his treasure. When Jesus is our portion, our hope is in Him and the life to come, and this is a hope that is eternal.

In Psalm 74, Asaph reflects on the destruction of the temple of Jerusalem during the Babylonian invasion. The temple represented God's presence with the people of Israel, so the loss of such would be devastating. And though Asaph questions the Lord and pleads with Him to destroy their enemies, he again recounts God's faithfulness and His power, and he asks the Lord to keep His covenant. The Lord will do so in Jesus. Soon, there will no longer be a need for the temple, because God will be present with His people through Jesus and then through the Holy Spirit!

"While we deserve to taste God's wrath and die, Jesus has tasted it upon the cross in our stead."

Psalm 75 calls us to recount the wondrous works of God and how the entire earth is in His hands. He is Sovereign over all who are lifted up and brought down. The psalm describes the wrath of God as pouring from a cup (Psalm 75:8), and while we deserve to taste God's wrath and die, Jesus has tasted it upon the cross in our stead. We are no longer cut off with the wicked but raised with the righteous.

QUESTIONS

Meditate on Psalm 73:28. Do you believe that God's presence is your good? What are some practical steps you can take to intentionally be nearer to God?

In Psalm 74:12 (ESV), Asaph says that God is "from ancient times." What do you think this means? The book of Daniel refers to God as the "Ancient of Days" (Daniel 7:9, 13, 22). How do you think these are connected, knowing that God has no beginning and no end?

Psalm 75 starts by giving thanks to God and thinking back to how He has been faithful. What are five "wondrous deeds" you have seen of the Lord in your own life this past week, whether it has been gratitude for your salvation or for His simple mercy in giving you a beautiful sunrise?

Psalms 76-80

Psalm 76 refers to God's defeat and slaying of 185,000 Assyrians (Isaiah 37:33-36). The Lord is a fierce and mighty warrior, but He is also personal and close to His people.

He makes His dwelling place with them. Psalm 76:10 describes the Lord putting on wrath against His enemies like a man puts on a belt. This is a picture of Jesus, the King of kings, who executes judgment against God's enemies (Daniel 10:5, Revelation 1:12-16).

Psalm 77 contains more heartfelt and honest cries from Asaph as he lets out all of his complaints to God. He still wonders if God has rejected His people, but as soon as he appeals to the Lord and remembers God's faithfulness, Asaph is reminded of what is true (Psalm 77:10-12). He ends the psalm by giving a detailed description of the exodus when God delivered His people from slavery by parting the Red Sea (Exodus 14). We must also remember that God has been faithful to us. He has delivered us from the slavery of sin through the death and resurrection of Jesus!

In Psalm 78, Asaph admonishes Israel to instruct their children about who God is and what He has done so that He would be their Lord and they would hope and trust in Him. Asaph does not want to see future generations repeat the mistakes of their fathers. We are also responsible for instructing the generations who come after us—that they would understand the story of Scripture and how God has redeemed His people. He is a compassionate God who atoned for our iniquity by the blood of His own Son, Jesus, the promised King from the line of Judah. All generations must know His name!

Psalm 79 is considered a companion psalm to Psalm 74, which also deals with the fall of Jerusalem to the Babylonians. The psalm gives detailed descriptions of the destruction of the holy city, but it also laments the sins of the people who caused it to occur. Asaph and the people cry out, "How long, Lord?" (Psalm 79:5). We, too, cry out these words, though we read this psalm knowing that God has delivered His people from sin through Jesus. We still see evil and the presence of sin in the world, and we groan with creation and wait with the people of God for our King to return.

Psalm 80 contains yet another lament from Asaph, but it is also a pleading for restoration. In many ways, this psalm looks ahead to the coming Messiah, who

"Jesus is our tender shepherd King who will restore His people to Himself."

170

would be everything humanity could not be. The psalm begins by speaking of God as the Good Shepherd of Israel, and though this is a common name for the Lord throughout the Bible, it is the only other time in Psalms that it is used other than in Psalm 23. Jesus claims this title in John 10, and He goes on to say that He will lay down His life for the sheep. Jesus is our tender shepherd King who will restore His people to Himself.

QUESTIONS

Psalm 77 begins with great grief from the psalmist, but we see a change in verse 11. How does this psalm teach you to remember the goodness of God when going through suffering?

In Psalm 79:13, the psalmist uses the imagery of God's people as sheep in a pasture. What are some parallels you see between Christians and sheep? Likewise, how is God like a shepherd to us?

We read the plea, "restore us" three times in Psalm 80. What does it mean for God to restore us?

Psalms 81-85

As a reminder, covenant language is the vernacular used to express God's relationship to Israel and all of His creation. Here it is used as a reminder that if they obey the Lord and do not turn aside to other gods and idols, He will bless them and deliver them from their enemies. Try as they might, Israel would never perfectly follow God. But God in His compassion would come in the person of Jesus to fulfill the law and obey it perfectly, giving God's people His righteousness. Our God accomplishes for us what we could never do on our own, and He fully satisfies all of our needs and desires in Christ (Psalm 81:16).

Asaph uses both lament and prophecy in Psalm 82 as he mourns the wicked rulers of the earth and points readers to the future judgment of God. God appoints human rulers to lead with righteousness, but these rulers often do the opposite of what God intended. We have only to look at the history of the world to see how many human kings and leaders have oppressed the poor and needy and used their power for evil. While human authorities may fail, God does not, and He will judge the earth in righteousness. The nations will someday be under the perfect rule of Jesus when He returns to the earth.

Psalm 83 is the last of Asaph's psalms, and it contains both lament and a call for God to destroy Israel's enemies. Asaph describes how numerous nations have joined forces against God's people, and he calls on the Lord to destroy them. Throughout Israel's history in the Old Testament, nation after nation tried to annihilate them, but God always delivered them. God preserved Israel and brought forth His Son through the line of Judah. Because of Jesus, we also can trust God to deliver us from our enemies. We live in a world that is hostile toward the gospel, but the truth of Jesus will always prevail.

Psalm 84 begins a series of psalms attributed to the Sons of Korah. The Sons of Korah were Levites who mainly served to provide music for temple worship (2 Chronicles 20:19). In Psalm 84, they beautifully describe their longing for the Lord's courts and His presence. To be with the Lord is the answer to the emptiness in every human soul. The Sons of Korah say that one day with God in His courts is better than a thousand elsewhere. We can have deep joy in knowing that we will be with God forever because of Jesus.

"The righteousness of Christ covers our sin so that we can be at peace with God."

The Sons of Korah plead with God in Psalm 85 to complete His redemptive work and bring restoration and revival to the people of Israel. In verse 10, the psalmist refers to the coming salvation of the Lord and says, "Faithful love and truth will join together; righteousness and peace will embrace." This verse is a picture of what will happen on the cross as Jesus gives His life for God's chosen people. The righteousness of Christ covers our sin so that we can be at peace with God. We have truly experienced the faithful, steadfast love of God.

QUESTIONS

Meditate on Colossians 3:2. In what ways can the book of Psalms help you set your mind on things above?

Reread Psalm 84:10-12. In what ways do these verses help you to have an eternal mindset rather than an earthly one?

Focus on Psalm 85:10-13. How do these verses grow your understanding of the character of God?

Psalms 86-90

Psalm 86 is a song of David, and it is anchored in what God says about Himself to Moses in Exodus 34:6-7: "The Lord — the Lord is a compassionate and gracious God, slow to anger and abounding in faithful love and truth, maintaining faithful love to a thousand generations, forgiving iniquity, rebellion, and sin."

Because David knows this truth about the Lord and His love, he knows he can come before the Lord and ask Him for help. God's faithful love is most fully expressed in Jesus, and we can confidently petition the Lord and enter into His presence because Jesus has made a way for us to do so.

The city of God, "Zion," is the subject of Psalm 87. While Zion first refers to the Lord's dwelling with His people in the temple in Jerusalem, the city of God will ultimately be fulfilled at the end of time when Jesus returns to earth, and all of God's people are restored to Him again (Revelation 21:3). There will even be people from Israel's enemies who are "reborn" as citizens of Zion. We are reborn as citizens of Zion, adopted sons and daughters of God, because of Christ.

Psalm 88 is the last psalm attributed to one of the Sons of Korah, Heman the Ezrahite. From the times he is mentioned in Scripture, we know he was accomplished, wise, and blessed by God (1 Kings 4:31, 1 Chronicles 6:33, 1 Chronicles 25:5-6). And yet, he still experienced times of deep despair. His psalm is known as being the darkest in the entire psalter. It even ends with the word "darkness," and yet it points us to Christ. When Heman cries out to God and asks Him if He "works wonders for the dead," we know that He most certainly does! Because Christ is resurrected, we will also be resurrected, for death is not the end.

Psalm 89 is still a lament like Psalm 88, but it is filled with praise and hope in who God is rather than darkness and hopelessness. The psalmist praises God and then recounts the covenant made with David. The psalmist then shifts his tone in verse 38 to cry out about Israel's current hardship. Though the people of God did not understand how He would fulfill His covenant, the Lord would do more than they could imagine through Jesus. In our hardship, we must remember the Lord's steadfast, faithful love He has shown us through His Son and let it fortify our trust in God.

"We will find true wisdom and joy as Christ consumes our thoughts and affections."

Psalm 90 is the first psalm of the fourth book of Psalms. It is a psalm of Moses, and it is likely that the children of Israel prayed and sung the words as they wandered in the wilderness after their redemption from Egypt. As the people of Israel wandered, they were reminded again and again that God was their dwelling place, and the earth was not. When we realize the brevity of our lives and often think about eternity and our hope in Christ, we will find true wisdom and joy as Christ consumes our thoughts and affections.

QUESTIONS

Spend some time meditating on Psalm 86:11. What does it mean to have an undivided heart to fear His name?

Psalm 89:1-4 reminds us of the covenant between God and David and His love for the people of Israel. Why might it be important to remind ourselves of the promises that God has given to us?

In Psalm 90:4, the psalmist says that a thousand years are only like a few hours to God. How does this truth of God inform the time you spend here on earth?

Psalms 91-95

We can trust Him to be with us and deliver us. We do not need to fear any-thing, for we are covered and protected by His love. As a mother bird pulls her babies close and covers them in the shelter of her wings, so our God will do for us. When evil spirals around us, we will be safe in His arms. Nothing can separate us from the love of God in Christ (Romans 8:38-39).

The Sabbath was a weekly day of rest God instructed the Israelites to follow under the Mosaic covenant, and Psalm 92 gives us an example of a song they would sing as they reflected on the steadfast love and faithfulness of God each week during this day of rest. Even though believers today are under the new covenant and are no longer required to keep the Sabbath, regular rest in God is a wise rhythm to practice. When we rest in God and put aside our work, we are reminded of who He is and our eternal rest that is coming because of Christ (Hebrews 4:1-11).

Psalm 93 declares the majesty and kingship of God. The Lord reigns above all the heavens and earth, and this should make our hearts leap for joy, for we worship and know a great King. Because of Jesus, we have become His adopted children, and we are covered in His love. There are no storms or waves of the sea that are mightier than the Lord. They are mere shadows of His power, so as the events of our life shake us, we can rely on the King who will never be shaken.

When the enemies of God seem to prevail, we may be tempted to think that God has forsaken us, but this is never the case. In Psalm 94, the psalmist cries out against the enemies of God and asks Him to "rise up, Judge of the earth" (Psalm 94:2). God will defend His people, and He will always be their help. We are not to take vengeance into our own hands because God has told us that He will accomplish it on our behalf (Romans 12:19). The vengeance of God should fall on us because we were once His enemies, but we now feel the love and protection of God because of Jesus. And when Jesus returns, He will judge the living and the dead, and the wicked will not be able to hide from Him (2 Timothy 4:1).

"In Christ, we have been given the greatest joy."

Continuing through Psalms, Psalm 95 is a beautiful call for followers of God to worship Him. It combines elements of reminding believers who God is and instructing them in the manner of what worship should look like. The Lord deserves the devotion of our hearts. He is a great God and a great King, and He has made us "the sheep under His care" (Psalm 95:7). He lovingly watches over us. In Christ, we have been given the greatest joy, and our expression of this joy should be heartfelt and exuberant worship.

QUESTIONS

Reread Psalm 92:14. What would it look like to still bear fruit for the kingdom of God in your old age? Spend some time in prayer, asking that God would make your life fruitful for Him.

Psalm 94:12 speaks to the importance of discipline. Do you have a heartfelt desire for the Lord to instruct you and discipline you? Why is it important for these things to take place?

Psalm 95 is a psalm praising God for His greatness. What are some aspects of God's character found in this psalm?

Psalms 96-100

God's glory will be known by His people, all of the nations, and even creation itself.

Psalms 96 and 97 show us a picture of how the good news of the gospel will touch every people group and corner of the earth. Believers of Jesus are messengers of this good news to the world, but one day the whole world will worship God. And when Jesus returns, all of creation will worship Him, proclaim His coming, and rejoice. The earth waits with eager expectation for Christ's return when all will be made right (Romans 8:19-23). We pursue righteousness now in anticipation of the day when God's reign will be seen upon all the earth.

Psalm 98 echoes much of Psalm 96, but it further emphasizes to Israel that they are God's chosen people who He will use to reach the entire world. The song Mary sings after the birth of Christ sounds very similar to this psalm, which may indicate that Mary understood that Jesus was its fulfillment (Luke 1:45-56). When we look at the beginning verses, we see hints of the Messiah. The Lord's right hand has worked salvation for Him, referring to Jesus's life, death, and resurrection, and this salvation has been revealed to all the earth. When Christ's kingdom is finally visible at His return, the earth will be reborn, and there will no longer be any curse. Everyone and everything will rejoice as God and His people are finally restored to each other (Revelation 22:3).

Psalm 99 calls us to recognize God's holiness. The psalmist says three times that the Lord is holy, which reminds us of Isaiah's future vision of the Lord in which the cherubim call out to each other and say that He is "Holy, Holy, Holy" (Isaiah 6:3). This psalm also mentions the cherubim and the Lord sitting enthroned between them (Psalm 99:1). God's holiness defines everything about who He is, and it makes Him entirely different than us. However, though He is high above us, He has also chosen to come near to us. He forgave us and sent Jesus to pay the penalty for our wrongdoings so that we could worship the Lord forever and have fellowship with Him (Psalm 99:8-9).

Psalm 100 is titled as a song of thanksgiving and gives the people several ways to show the Lord gratitude, many of those ways involving worship and

"Indeed we have been shown the steadfast love of the Lord!"

178

praise. The last verse of this short psalm declares the Lord's steadfast love and faithfulness to all generations, which is fulfilled in the work of Christ and should bring joy to believers. Following Christ brings us deep happiness, even when we face difficult circumstances, for indeed we have been shown the steadfast love of the Lord!

QUESTIONS

How does Psalm 98 prompt you to respond to the steadfast love of God?

Psalm 99 praises God for the works He did for Moses, Aaron, and Samuel. In what ways can you praise God for the works He has done for Israel?

Dwell on Psalm 100, and spend some time in prayer, reading through this psalm and praising God. Play some of your favorite worship music, and imagine someday being before the throne of God forever.

Psalms 101-105

While this psalm describes the kind of rule David wanted to have as king, it is ultimately a depiction and foreshadowing of the future messianic King, Jesus. Only Jesus could fulfill the words of this psalm as He is the only one who is blameless, and He alone knows nothing of evil (Psalm 101:1-4). Jesus will dwell with His covenant people in His future kingdom, and He will completely cut off the enemies of God (Psalm 101:6-8). He is the only King who reigns with perfect integrity.

Psalm 102 contains the words of a person in deep affliction. It describes Jerusalem (Zion) as lying in ruin, so we can assume that this may have been written during the exile. The psalmist describes his loss of strength and appetite and his feelings of loneliness and sorrow. However, while he reflects on his mortality, he is reminded that God is enthroned forever. The author of Hebrews quotes the last few verses of this psalm to describe Jesus Himself. Heaven and earth will pass away, but Jesus will never pass away (Psalm 102:25-27). One day God will restore Jerusalem (Zion), and He will bring His redeemed people to worship Him there forever.

Psalm 103 is the second psalm attributed to David in the fourth book of the psalter, and he calls us to bless the Lord because He is our Great Redeemer! David beautifully portrays the gospel in his words. The Lord has forgiven all of our iniquities and redeemed our lives from the pit of sin because of Christ's life, death, and resurrection (Psalm 103:3-4). He has placed His steadfast love on us, and He has removed all of our sins (Psalm 103:11-12). The Lord is truly our gracious and compassionate Father.

Psalm 104 shows us the glory of God revealed in His creation. This psalm should cause us to pause, look out our windows, and recognize that the earth is the work of the Lord's hands, and He is intimately involved with everything in it. The Lord is high above us, but He also sustains all of creation. As we reflect on this truth, we find awe in that the Lord created all things through Christ, and in Christ, all things are upheld and sustained (Hebrews 1:2-3). Christ cares for all of creation, and all of creation is dependent upon Him.

Psalm 105 reminds us that God keeps His covenant. The first fifteen verses of this psalm can also be read in 1 Chronicles when David celebrates the

"We read this psalm knowing that our salvation is possible because God keeps His covenants."

return of the ark to Jerusalem. So while he is not named the author, we can assume that he was the one who wrote it. The psalmist tells of the wondrous works of God by writing a poem capturing the history of God's people and how He has kept His covenant with Abraham. We read this psalm knowing that our salvation is possible because God keeps His covenants. He has allowed us to be a part of His redeemed people under a new covenant in Christ (Hebrews 10:15-25).

QUESTIONS

Highlight or make a list of each verse or phrase in Psalm 103 that points forward to the gospel. How does seeing the gospel in the Old Testament remind you of the Lord's love?

Reflect on Psalm 104:34, and then read Joshua 1:8, Psalm 1:2, and Psalm 19:14. To what kind of meditation do you think the psalmist is referring?

Psalm 105 outlines many of God's wonderful works throughout the Old Testament. How does reading about the redemptive work of God encourage you in your Christian walk?

Psalms 106-110

Psalm 106 recounts a condensed history of Israel that displays God's faithfulness and Israel's forgetfulness.

The Lord took care of His people every step of the way, and they continued to rebel against Him. And yet, even in their rejection, He was faithful and kept His covenant (Psalm 106:44-45). As the redeemed of the Lord, we can rejoice and praise Him for pursuing us even when we have also been unfaithful and blind to our sin. And when we continue to struggle with sin and temptation as followers of Christ, His love is steadfast, and "he gives greater grace" (James 4:6).

Psalm 107 begins the fifth and final book of Psalms, and it continues with the themes we see in Psalms 105 and 106. Even when God's people rebel against Him, He restores them and has mercy. Psalm 107 offers different scenarios from which the Lord redeems His people: He delivers them from wandering in the wilderness, captivity, sickness, and the dangerous seas. The psalm prompts the people to praise the Lord and offer Him songs and sacrifices of thankfulness. We have also experienced God's deliverance and have seen Him faithfully intervene on our behalf. May we be known for our gratitude to Him for giving us salvation through Jesus.

Psalm 108 is a plea from David to the Lord to deliver the people from their enemies. Though the Lord seems absent from their struggle, David's hope is in God, and he sings of God's love and faithfulness (Psalm 108:1, 4). David knows that God has promised to always be with Israel (Psalm 108:7-9). David gives a prophecy from the Lord that declares Judah will always have the scepter (Genesis 49:10). We have seen this promise before, and we know that Jesus, the messianic King, is the fulfillment of it! He will be the one who will provide God's ultimate display and means of salvation through the cross, and He will tread down the enemies of God forever.

Psalm 109 is another Imprecatory Psalm. Commentators refer to this as the strongest one in the entire psalter. Wicked men surround David, cursing him and hating him, even though he has only shown them love (Psalm 109:1-5). In many ways, the treatment David receives reminds us of how Christ was treated throughout his time on earth. Even though David calls down curses on his enemies, he knew he was to leave vengeance to the Lord. In light of Jesus's teaching on how we should treat our enemies, we

"May we be known for our gratitude to Him for giving us salvation through Jesus."

know that we should not curse them as David did but love them and forgive them (Matthew 5:43-44). We can only do this in Christ's strength.

Psalm 110 contains the promise of a Messiah from the Lord to the people of Israel. The first line of the psalm makes it clear that the Lord is not speaking to David but another divine figure (Psalm 110:1). This coming deliverer would not only be the true King, but He would also be their Great High Priest. In the Old Testament, the high priest was the only one allowed into the Holy of Holies, where God dwelled. And the Lord says the deliverer would be from the line of Melchizedek, the priest who was also king of Salem and a king of peace and righteousness like Jesus. David wrote this psalm and looked forward to His coming, and now we can read it and look back to Jesus's life, knowing that He fulfilled David's prophecy.

QUESTIONS

Reread Psalm 107:2. What does it mean to let the redeemed of the Lord "proclaim that he has redeemed them from the power of the foe"? In what ways can we proclaim daily what the Lord has done for us?

How does Psalm 109 encourage you to rely on the help of the Lord? How does it grow your trust in God's plan?

In what ways does Psalm 110 point you toward Christ and grow your affections for Him?

Psalms 111–115

Psalm 111 and 112 are both acrostic poems. This means that each line in these psalms, except the beginning calls to praise the Lord, are successive letters in the Hebrew alphabet.

One commentator, James Montgomery Boice, noted that these two psalms are companions: Psalm 111 is an acrostic about the works of God, and Psalm 112 is an acrostic about the righteousness of man. Psalm 111 continues with the repeated theme in the psalms of remembering the wondrous works of God. And it is true that the more we remember and study what the Lord has done, the more in awe of Him we will become. Similarly, the more we reflect upon the gospel of Jesus, the more we will love our Savior. And this love for Him changes us. Truly, "the fear of the Lord is the beginning of wisdom" (Psalm 111:10).

Psalm 112 gives us an example of a godly man who practices remembering the works of God mentioned in Psalm 111. And while many godly men in the Bible could certainly fit some of the descriptions provided in this psalm, the only one who is perfectly "gracious and compassionate" is Christ (Psalm 111:4). And He is the only one who "will be remembered forever" (Psalm 112:6). Christ is our example of how to live our lives in response to what God has done. And while we seek to become more like Him, we can rest in His righteousness, knowing that He has accomplished salvation for us, and in that, we can enjoy Him forever (Psalm 112:9).

Psalm 113-118 are all songs that the Jews sang in celebration of Passover each year. Psalm 113 reminds us that God is infinitely above us, and there is no one like Him. And yet, our great God cares for the lowly and poor creatures of His creation. He even thinks of the barren women who cry out to Him for children, and He satisfies their longing (1 Samuel 2:1-10). We are just like a barren woman, unable to change our condition, and yet God has opened our eyes to the truth of the gospel. He has fulfilled the longing of our hearts with Himself. Psalm 114 reminds Israel of when the Lord delivered them from the Egyptians by parting the Red Sea. The psalmist goes on to emphasize that the Lord is sovereign over nature (Psalm 114:7-8). When Jesus comes to earth, He shows His disciples that He is God by displaying His control over nature by calming the winds and the waves. This was something that they would know was a characteristic of God because they sang these psalms each year.

"He has fulfilled the longing of our hearts with Himself."

Psalm 115 reminds us that we do not seek our own glory but the glory of the Lord. This life is not about us; it is about Him. We are not trying to build up our name but are trying to magnify His name. We should live each day pointing to our Savior and seeking to build His kingdom but not our own. This end of the psalm reminds us of the words of John the Baptist in John 3:30, "He must increase, but I must decrease." May this be our prayer today and every day.

QUESTIONS

Meditate on Psalm 112:7-8. What does it mean to have a heart that is confident and assured? How can we obtain a confident and assured heart?

Reread Psalm 114:7-8 and think about the imagery used. What does knowing that creation trembled at the presence of the Lord teach us about God?

In what ways does John 3:30 help you better understand Psalm 115?

Psalms 116-120

Psalm 116 describes the condition of every human being before God intervenes on our behalf.

We are destined for hell and destruction, but God saves us from death by giving us salvation in Jesus. When we pass away from this life, death will only take our broken bodies, but if we are believers, our souls will be delivered to Jesus, and we will "walk before the Lord in the land of the living" (Psalm 116:9). The psalmist's response to redemption is public praise of the Lord and proclaiming that his salvation is from God (Psalm 116:13-14, 17-18). We do not need to fear death because, as Charles Spurgeon says, "it is the doorway to an eternity of perfect fellowship."

Psalm 117 is just several verses, but it is nonetheless powerful. All the world is to praise the Lord because He has made a way for salvation for His people, and they will be from every nation. God models His love for His people to the nation of Israel throughout the Old Testament. However, His intention has always been to gather people from every tribe and nation. And we are part of this gathering in Christ.

The psalmist begins Psalm 118 with a call to worship the Lord because of His steadfast love. This call is directed to the people of Israel, the priests, and even Gentiles who fear Him (Psalm 118:2-4). The psalmist then gives the people encouragement from personal testimony of the Lord's faithfulness. Even when man was against the psalmist, he put his trust in the Lord. Nation after nation was against the people of Israel, but the Lord delivered them and saved them. Though Israel was meant to guide the nations to a knowledge of the Lord and salvation in Him, they were the first "stone" that the builders, or the surrounding nations, rejected (Psalm 118:22). Jesus will later use this verse to describe Himself, but the nation of Israel will reject Him as the cornerstone of God's plan of salvation for them and all of the world (Matthew 21:42).

Psalm 119 is the longest in the psalter, and it is another acrostic poem that contains each letter of the Hebrew alphabet at the beginning of each stanza. It describes the beauty of the Word of God. God's Word brings life, and it is our comfort and guide. Scripture is true, trustworthy, and timeless. It

"Jesus is the King of peace and righteousness."

reminds us of God's goodness in all things, and it fills our hearts with love for our God. Jesus is the embodiment of God's Word to us (John 1:14), for everything true about God's Word is true about Him.

Psalm 120 begins a series of psalms called "The Song of Ascents." While we do not know exactly how these songs were used, most commentators speculate that the Israelites sang them as they journeyed to Jerusalem to the temple for the Feasts of Passover, Pentecost, and Tabernacles. In Psalm 120, the psalmist is in distress because he is away from the people of God and amidst unfriendly, hostile nations. He desires peace, but the nations he is with desire war. They also are full of deception. Jesus is the King of peace and righteousness, and He dwelt among people who were sinful and wanted destruction. He models for us what it looks like to be a citizen of heaven on the earth, and He allows us to be citizens of heaven through His sacrifice on the cross.

QUESTIONS

Meditate on Psalm 118:24. In what ways does this encourage you to use your days wisely and rejoice in the Lord, despite troubles you may face?

Spend some time in prayer, praying through Psalm 119:169 and asking that God would continually help you understand and discern His Word.

The first verse in Psalm 120 shows the psalmist calling to God in distress. Is God the first one you call on when you are experiencing distress? Why might it be important to plead your case to Him?

Psalms 121-125

Psalm 121 continues the "Songs of Ascents." The psalmist depicts traveling to Jerusalem and trusting in the Lord throughout the journey.

Pilgrims would sing this every year as they climbed the steep hills to arrive at the covenant city, and even though the way could be dangerous, they trusted in the Lord who would be their "Protector" and their "shelter" by their side (Psalm 121:4-5). When we are in Christ, we know that the Lord is the shelter for our life, like this psalm says. He will always be with us, and He will keep our souls from evil. He will be us to the very end of this life and into all of eternity.

Psalm 122 shows that the psalmist and other pilgrims who sang this song have now arrived in Jerusalem, and they are happy to be in the city of God where His presence dwells with His people. This psalm emphasizes God's promise that He made to David to establish his throne forever. Even though there would seemingly be an end to the line of Israel's kings and chaos in the holy city as Jerusalem was destroyed by the Babylonians, we know that Jesus is the fulfillment of David's line and the embodiment of peace to the covenant people of God.

Now that the people are in Jerusalem, they set their gaze and worship on the Lord, and they plead with Him for mercy. Psalm 123 shows the people's distress over the contempt and scorn from their enemies and the world around them. However, it is important to note that the psalmist begins by stating that the Lord is "enthroned in heaven" (Psalm 123:1). We are also subjected to scorn and contempt from the world as followers of Jesus, but our hope is always in our enthroned Lord. We have His love, and we are under His care. That is enough.

Psalm 124 is a Song of Ascents written by David, and it continues with the theme of relying on God for deliverance. David calls the covenant people to sing of how the Lord has always been on their side, and the psalm gives specific examples of what would have happened if He was not. Satan hates God's redeemed people, so much so that he tried to destroy Israel, and He also tries to divide and destroy the Church today; but our God delivers us! If He had not intervened for us before we became His sons and daughters, we would have been destroyed, but we are given new life!

"We belong to the eternal city of Zion, and we will abide with the Lord forever."

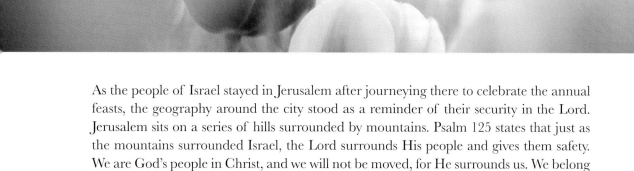

As the people of Israel stayed in Jerusalem after journeying there to celebrate the annual feasts, the geography around the city stood as a reminder of their security in the Lord. Jerusalem sits on a series of hills surrounded by mountains. Psalm 125 states that just as the mountains surrounded Israel, the Lord surrounds His people and gives them safety. We are God's people in Christ, and we will not be moved, for He surrounds us. We belong to the eternal city of Zion, and we will abide with the Lord forever (Psalm 125:1).

QUESTIONS

Meditate on Psalm 121:1-2. Why is it important to dwell on the fact that our help comes from the Lord? Is this something you have trouble remembering?

Reread Psalm 125:1. What does it mean that we are like Mount Zion? What are some ways that we can trust God more fully?

Choose a psalm from today's reading, and spend some time meditating on the words and praying them to God.

Psalms 126-130

Psalm 126 is the seventh of fifteen songs that the people of God sang as they came to Jerusalem for the annual observance of their pilgrimage festivals.

It is a song of God's restoration and most likely speaks of the restoration of the people from exile. It also speaks of the people's longing for future restoration as we too long for future restoration. God has redeemed us by Christ's blood, but we await Christ's return to bring complete restoration to the earth and to defeat death and sin. The first few verses of this psalm could be said to foreshadow what it will be like for God's people when Christ returns—and when that day comes, though it may feel like a dream, the joy found in that moment of full restoration will never end!

Psalm 127 is a Song of Ascents that Solomon wrote. Solomon's psalm gives a timeless message to the people that all of their labor, whether it be on houses, cities, or in creating families, is in vain if they are working from their strength and not the Lord's. Human beings often run from rest and act as if their weakness does not limit them, but rest is a precious gift from the Lord that He gives to us because He loves us and desires to sustain us. Jesus modeled resting in God by regularly meeting with Him in the quiet to pray. We are utterly dependent on God, and that is a beautiful thing.

Psalm 128 reminds the people of Israel that everyone who fears the Lord is blessed. God graciously allows His people to be saved, and then He uses their love and fear for Him as a way to bless others who may not know Him. The life of believers in Christ leads to their flourishing as well as the flourishing of others. This does not necessarily mean flourishing in terms of earthly prosperity but a flourishing of the soul. Our love for God will impact generations after us.

In Psalm 129, the psalmist remembers the severe affliction that Israel has continuously felt from their enemies, but the psalmist uses this affliction to show God's faithfulness. Israel's enemies never prevailed, even when all appeared to be hopeless. God always delivered His people. We see the enemies of God come against His people still today, but we know that they will not prevail. Jesus will put all of the enemies of God under His feet, and He will bring God's people into eternal rest with Him.

"It is a sweet comfort to know that He pours out His mercy and grace to cover our sin."

190

Psalm 130 is a psalm of lament. The psalmist first reflects on his sin, but then in the latter half of the psalm, he calls Israel to remember that the Lord has redeemed Israel from all of their iniquities. Psalm 130 proclaims rich gospel truth. If the Lord judged us based on our iniquities, no one could stand before Him, but He has given us forgiveness through the blood of Jesus (Psalm 130:3-4). It is a sweet comfort to know that He pours out His mercy and grace to cover our sin. In us, there is sin, but in Him, there is plentiful, abundant redemption (Psalm 130:7).

QUESTIONS

Spend some time reflecting on Psalm 127:1. Why does someone labor in vain when they work apart from God?

In Psalm 128, we see the connection between fearing the Lord and walking in His ways. How does this psalm help deepen your understanding of what it means to fear the Lord?

Reread Psalm 130:5-6. How can this passage be a comfort in your seasons of waiting?

Psalms 131-135

Psalm 131 is another Song of Ascent written by David. He creates a beautiful picture of what it looks like to fear God and have your heart quieted in Him.

David knows that the Lord is high above Him, and there are things he will never understand because they are "too great or too wondrous" for him, but they are not so for God (Psalm 131:1). David's humility leads to a rested heart in the Lord, and he compares himself to a weaned child with his mother, who is comforted by her caring and loving presence. We have become children of God, and we too can rest in Him while knowing that His love is deeper than that of any earthly relationship we have. There is a tenderness from our Father toward us. This should prompt a tenderness within us toward our heavenly Father.

Psalm 132 reminds the people of Israel of the covenant God made to David in 2 Samuel 7. Throughout the psalms, we see a foreshadowing of how God will fulfill this covenant. As the people of Israel sang this song during their pilgrimage journey to Jerusalem, they would remember the life of David and look forward to the fulfillment of God's promise. We know that Jesus is the "offspring" of David that the Lord will set on his throne (Psalm 132:11). Jesus will reign forever, and Zion will be where God dwells with all of the redeemed. It is the heavenly home for which we long.

Psalm 133 is another psalm written by David, and it speaks of the importance of brotherly unity. He describes brotherly unity as "good and pleasant" and provides two follow-up illustrations. When the people of God are united, it is holy and sacred, like anointing oil that is used by the priests. David also compares brotherly unity to the "dew of Hermon." Dew in a land that is made up primarily of desert indicates life and flourishing. When we are united with our brothers and sisters in Christ, it leads to refreshment and nourishment for the entire body of Christ. The unity we experience now will be fully expressed when the redeemed people of the Lord are united forever in heaven.

Psalm 134 is the last Song of Ascent and calls the priests to bless the Lord. As the people leave Jerusalem and journey back to their homes, the priests stay in the house of God and represent the people to Him. They bless the Lord and then speak blessings to the people. We never have to leave the presence of God,

"He alone is worthy of their adoration, and His name will be known forever."

for He is with us always through His Spirit. When we bless or praise Him, we can speak directly to Him. Believers have become a "royal priesthood" in Jesus Christ (1 Peter 2:9).

Psalm 135 is a call to Israel to praise the Lord, for He has chosen them for His possession. It reminds the people that He is in complete control of the world and all of its circumstances, and there is no other like Him. He alone is worthy of their adoration, and His name will be known forever. God extended His covenant of mercy and love to the Gentiles through Christ, and now we also are under the care of this powerful, sovereign God.

QUESTIONS

Meditate on Psalm 131. What does this psalm teach you about a calm and quiet soul? Would you say this is the state of your soul?

Psalm 133 draws attention to the goodness of dwelling in unity with one another. How might you seek out more unity with the body of Christ?

Reread Psalm 135:6. In what ways is it comforting to know that God does as He pleases?

Psalms 136–140

The Hebrew word being used in this phrase is *hesed*, and it often refers to the covenant love of God. Everything that God does is an expression of His faithful love. The fullest expression of the Lord's covenant love is in Jesus Christ, the Savior of the world, sent to die for the people of God. We represent the Lord's faithful love to the world every day as He allows us to live and fellowship with Him.

Psalm 137 contains the heartbreaking cries of the people of Israel after they are exiled. The psalmist gives a picture of the people sitting on the great rivers of Babylon, mourning their losses and the horror they saw as their temple, homes, and families were destroyed. The people ask the Lord to act against their enemies, and they say whoever dashes their enemies' children against the rocks will be blessed. This is strong language, but most likely, they have just seen their own children horrifically killed, and they desire retribution. However, they depend on the Lord to carry this punishment out Himself, and He will. Edom and Babylon were destroyed and are no more, but God faithfully preserved His covenant people, and He would eventually bring them a deliverer.

Many commentators note a sharp contrast between Psalm 137 and Psalm 138. While Psalm 137 shows a people who have no song left to sing to the Lord, Psalm 138 shows David praising God exuberantly and desiring the whole earth to sing the praises of God! The words of this psalm offer hope to the distress we saw in the last psalm. God will increase His people's strength (Psalm 138:3). He will preserve them and save them (Psalm 138:7). He will fulfill His purposes for His people (Psalm 138:8). Though we will surely find trouble in this world, Jesus will be with us, and He will use everything that we face for His glory and our good.

In Psalm 139, David describes the intimate relationship between himself and the Lord. The Lord sees and knows everything about David. He even knew David before he was born because the Lord formed him in the womb. And the same is true for us. The Lord knows the depths of our hearts. We are sinful people, and yet He loves us with steadfast love and showers us in mercy and grace that we do not deserve. Because of Jesus, we can have intimate fellowship with God and can confidently ask the Lord to search us and make us more like Him.

In Psalm 140, David cries to God to deliver him from the violent and wicked who surround him. It is similar to other psalms David has written on the same subject. David's troubles with these evil men compares to Jesus's struggle with those who plotted against Him, and again, while David brings curses upon His enemies, Jesus will pray for them. But both David and Jesus know that the Lord will act on behalf of them, and one day all who trust in Christ will be in His presence for all of eternity (Psalm 140:12-13).

QUESTIONS

Spend some time considering Psalm 138:7-8. How can dwelling on this verse grow your trust and faith in the Lord?

In what ways does Psalm 139 comfort you with how you are known by God?

How does Psalm 140:12 expand your understanding that God is just?

Psalms 141-145

"The Lord has shown us steadfast mercy and love."

He does not want to follow in the footsteps of the wicked, but he knows that he is capable of doing so. He asks the Lord for correction and rebuke from the righteous and compares this correction to healing oil. We are all capable of the worst kinds of sins because sin is a part of our fallen, human nature. Praise God for His intervention in our lives that allows us to see the truth of the gospel! And praise God that He continues to train us in righteousness as we will continue our struggle against sin until we see Him face to face.

Psalm 142 refers to a time when David hid from his enemies in a cave. It could very well have been when he was running for his life from Saul's court (1 Samuel 24). David desperately needs the Lord's help. He knows that his enemies are too strong for him and that His only defense and refuge is the Lord. The words of this psalm point us to the gospel. We are helpless in our sin without the Lord, but He saves us from the prison of death, and He delivers us to life through Jesus; He leads us into righteousness (Psalm 142:7).

In Psalm 143, David repeats the problem that humanity faces—no one is righteous. He seeks God, the only righteous one, and asks the Lord to act on his behalf. David remembers the Lord's past acts of faithfulness and is comforted. He knows that the Lord will show him steadfast love. It is good for us to see David struggle and respond in faith to the Lord. When we follow Jesus, we will not have a life of ease, but we have a Heavenly Father who sustains us and is our refuge. He will never leave us.

Psalm 144 is thought by many commentators to have been written when David ascended to the throne. This psalm speaks of times of war, peace, hardship, and blessing. David asks the Lord to be with him as king in all of these times and bless future generations who follow after him. He knows they will be blessed because the Lord is their God (Psalm 144:15). This psalm shows us that we can find comfort in knowing God is with us in every season of our lives. He is ours because Jesus has made a way for us to draw near to Him.

Psalm 145 is the last psalm of David in the psalter, and it beautifully praises the Lord. Commentator and theologian, James Montgomery Boice, says,

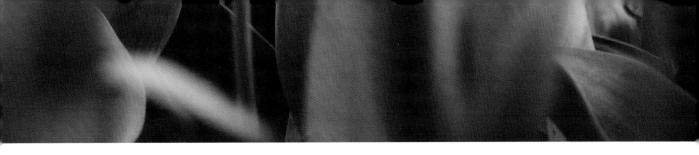

"Psalm 145 is indeed a monumental praise psalm, a fit summary of all David had learned about God during a long lifetime of following hard after the Almighty." Every word of this psalm is the rich inheritance of the believer. We have access to the Lord because of Jesus. The Lord has shown us steadfast mercy and love (Psalm 145:8-11). He has always been King; we are a part of His kingdom now, and we will be forever (Psalm 145:13).

QUESTIONS

In Psalm 141:3-4, we see David's plea to God to prohibit any unwholesome words from coming from his mouth. What does this illustrate to you about the power of the tongue?

In Psalm 144:12, David prays for the future generations of His kingdom. What is your prayer for the future generations of believers coming after you?

In what way(s) is Psalm 145 reflective of the gospel?

Psalms 146-150

The last five psalms of the psalter are known as the Hallelujah Psalms as each one ends with the phrase, "Hallelujah!"

Psalm 146 continues with the theme of the greatness of God, and it encourages the people not to put their trust in the rulers or authorities of the earth who are only men who will one day pass away and return to the dust of the earth. Thankfully, the Lord is forever. Verses 6-10 of this psalm point us to Christ. He is our perfect, good, and righteous King. We can place all of our hope in Him, and we can be confident that He will forever reign (Psalm 146:10).

Psalm 147 offers praise to God for His tender care of His people and all of creation. While God knows all of the stars in the heavens and names them, He also sees and cares for the heartbreak of His people (Psalm 147:3-4) and offers them healing. The Lord's power, majesty, and control over the earth lead us to praise Him, for He is infinitely trustworthy.

Psalm 148 calls all of creation to praise the Lord—from the angels in the heavens to the beasts that roam the earth. The Lord deserves praise from everything and everyone. This psalm points us to a day when all of the earth will praise the Lord. When Jesus returns, the words of Psalm 148 will finally be fulfilled. It is the moment for which all of our hearts long, whether we have accepted Jesus as Savior or not. As believers, this should move us immensely because we will one day see this psalm come to fruition.

Psalm 149 contains another song of praise to the Lord, and it calls Israel to celebrate and be glad in their Maker (Psalm 149:2). The psalm then tells us that "the Lord takes pleasure in his people" (Psalm 149:4). We delight in the Lord because the Lord first delighted in us, and when we become His children through Christ, the delight between the Lord and us only continues. However, our praise to Him is not only a means of joy; it also reveals those who do not love the Lord and obey Him. As believers go into the world praising God and speaking His Word, the enemies of God are revealed and judged by truth (Psalm 149:5-7).

Psalm 150 is the final psalm of the entire psalter, and just like the other four psalms that closed each of the five books in the psalter, this psalm is seen as a doxology. It calls the people of Israel to praise God in the sanctuary, and

"The Lord has shown us steadfast mercy and love."

while we no longer worship God in a temple today, we know that His presence is not limited by walls. God has put His presence in us through the Holy Spirit. We can praise Him everywhere because of the saving work of Christ. We have access to the majestic God the psalms glorify and honor again and again and again. He has done great things, and He has made a way for us to have salvation through Jesus. Everything with breath will one day praise Him. Let us demonstrate lives of praise to a broken world in desperate need of our Great God!

QUESTIONS

Reflect on Psalm 149:4. What does this verse teach you about God? What does this show you about the preciousness of salvation in Him?

What does Psalm 150 show you about praising God in all circumstances and all places?

Now that we have finished reading through the book of Psalms, what are some things that have impacted your relationship with God? How has your view of God been shaped by reading through this book?

What is the Gospel?

THANK YOU FOR READING AND ENJOYING THIS STUDY WITH US!
WE ARE ABUNDANTLY GRATEFUL FOR THE WORD OF GOD, THE INSTRUCTION
WE GLEAN FROM IT, AND THE EVER-GROWING UNDERSTANDING IT PROVIDES
FOR US OF GOD'S CHARACTER. WE ARE ALSO THANKFUL THAT SCRIPTURE
CONTINUALLY POINTS TO ONE THING IN INNUMERABLE WAYS: THE GOSPEL.

We remember our brokenness when we read about the fall of Adam and Eve in the garden of Eden (Genesis 3), when sin entered into a perfect world and maimed it. We remember the necessity that something innocent must die to pay for our sin when we read about the atoning sacrifices in the Old Testament. We read that we have all sinned and fallen short of the glory of God (Romans 3:23) and that the penalty for our brokenness, the wages of our sin, is death (Romans 6:23). We all are in need of grace and mercy, but most importantly, we all need a Savior.

We consider the goodness of God when we realize that He did not plan to leave us in this dire state. We see His promise to buy us back from the clutches of sin and death in Genesis 3:15. And we see that promise accomplished with Jesus Christ on the cross. Jesus Christ knew no sin yet became sin so that we might become righteous through His sacrifice (2 Corinthians 5:21). Jesus was tempted in every way that we are and lived sinlessly. He was reviled yet still yielded Himself for our sake, that we may have life abundant in Him. Jesus lived the perfect life that we could not live and died the death that we deserved.

The gospel is profound yet simple. There are many mysteries in it that we can never exhaust this side of heaven, but there is still overwhelming weight to its implications in this life. The gospel is the telling of our sinfulness and God's goodness, and this gracious gift compels a response. We are saved by grace through faith, which means

that we rest with faith in the grace that Jesus Christ displayed on the cross (Ephesians 2:8-9). We cannot save ourselves from our brokenness or do any amount of good works to merit God's favor, but we can have faith that what Jesus accomplished in His death, burial, and resurrection was more than enough for our salvation and our eternal delight. When we accept God, we are commanded to die to our self and our sinful desires and live a life worthy of the calling we have received (Ephesians 4:1). The gospel compels us to be sanctified, and in so doing, we are conformed to the likeness of Christ Himself. This is hope. This is redemption. This is the gospel.

SCRIPTURE TO REFERENCE:

GENESIS 3:15 — *I will put hostility between you and the woman, and between your offspring and her offspring. He will strike your head, and you will strike his heel.*

ROMANS 3:23 — *For all have sinned and fall short of the glory of God.*

ROMANS 6:23 — *For the wages of sin is death, but the gift of God is eternal life in Christ Jesus our Lord.*

2 CORINTHIANS 5:21 — *He made the one who did not know sin to be sin for us, so that in him we might become the righteousness of God.*

EPHESIANS 2:8-9 — *For you are saved by grace through faith, and this is not from yourselves; it is God's gift — not from works, so that no one can boast.*

EPHESIANS 4:1 — *Therefore I, the prisoner in the Lord, urge you to walk worthy of the calling you have received,*

Thank you for studying
God's Word with us!

CONNECT WITH US

@thedailygraceco

@kristinschmucker

CONTACT US

info@thedailygraceco.com

SHARE

#thedailygraceco

#lampandlight

VISIT US ONLINE

www.thedailygraceco.com

MORE DAILY GRACE

The Daily Grace App

Daily Grace Podcast